Grade 2

MW01093555

Assessment

Mc Graw Hill Education

Bothell, WA • Chicago, IL • Columbus, OH • New York, NY

Cover: Nathan Love

mheducation.com/prek-12

Send all inquiries to:
McGraw-Hill Education
Two Penn Plaza
New York, New York 10121

ISBN: 978-0-02-129954-6
MHID: 0-02-129954-4

Printed in the United States of America.

 6 7 8 9 10 11 LHS 21 20 19 18 17

D

TABLE OF CONTENTS

TABLE OF CONTENTS

Oral Reading Fluency Assessment

Scoring Sheets

Answer Keys

Assessment

The *Assessment* BLM is an integral part of the complete assessment program aligned with the core reading and intervention curriculums of *McGraw-Hill Reading WonderWorks* and *McGraw-Hill Reading Wonders*.

Purpose of *Assessment*

The instruction in *McGraw-Hill Reading WonderWorks* is parallel to the instruction in *McGraw-Hill Reading Wonders*. Results in *Assessment* provide a picture of achievement within *McGraw-Hill Reading WonderWorks* and a signal as to whether children can successfully transition back to Approaching Level reading instruction.

Assessment offers the opportunity to monitor progress in a steady and structured manner while providing formative assessment data.

As children complete each week of the intervention program, they will be assessed on their understanding of weekly vocabulary words and their ability to access and comprehend complex literary and informational selections using text evidence.

At the key 3-week and 6-week reporting junctures, assessments measure understanding of previously-taught vocabulary words and comprehension skills and provide evidence of progress through the curriculum. If children evidence a level of mastery at the end of a unit, an assessment to exit out of *McGraw-Hill Reading WonderWorks* and into the Approaching Level instruction of *McGraw-Hill Reading Wonders* is available.

Throughout the unit, oral reading fluency passages are available to measure the ability to read connected text fluently, accurately, and with a measure of prosody. The results of the assessments that comprise *Assessment* can be used to inform subsequent instruction and assist with grouping and leveling designations.

Components of *Assessment*

Assessment features the following tests:

- Weekly Assessment
- Mid-Unit Assessment
- Unit Assessment
- Exit Assessment
- Oral Reading Fluency Assessment

Assessment focuses on key areas of English Language Arts—Reading, Language, and Fluency. To assess Reading and Language proficiency, children read selections and respond to items focusing on comprehension skills, vocabulary words, literary elements, and text structures/features. These items assess the ability to access meaning from the text and demonstrate understanding of words and phrases. To assess Fluency, children read passages for one minute to measure their words correct per minute (WCPM) and accuracy rates.

Weekly Assessment

The Weekly Assessment features a "cold read" reading selection (informational or narrative based on the weekly reading focus) and 5 items—three items on the weekly comprehension skill and two items that ask children to show how context helps them identify the meaning of a vocabulary word. (For weeks in which poetry is the featured genre, vocabulary items are replaced by items assessing literary elements.) Children will provide text evidence to support their answers.

Administering Weekly Assessment

Each test should be administered once the instruction for the specific week is completed. Make a copy of the assessment and the Scoring Sheet for each child. The Scoring Sheet allows for informal comments on responses and adds to an understanding of strengths and weaknesses.

After each child has a copy of the assessment, provide a version of the following directions: **Say:** *Write your name and the date on the question pages for this assessment.* (When children are finished, continue with the directions.) *You will read a selection and answer questions about it. Read the selection and the questions that follow it carefully. Write your responses on the lines provided. Go back to the text to underline and circle the text evidence that supports your answers. When you have completed the assessment, put your pencil down and turn the pages over. You may begin now.*

Answer procedural questions during the assessment, but do not provide any assistance on the items or selections. After the class has completed the assessment, ask children to verify that their names and the date are written on the necessary pages.

Alternatively, you may choose to work through the assessment with the children. This will provide an additional opportunity for you to observe their ability to access complex text in a more informal group setting.

Evaluating the Weekly Assessment

Each Weekly Assessment is worth 10 points, with each item worth 2 points. Use the scoring rubric below to assign a point total per item. A Weekly Answer Key is provided to help with scoring. Children's results should provide a clear picture of their understanding of the weekly comprehension skill and the weekly vocabulary words. Reteach tested skills if assessment results point to a clear deficiency.

Weekly Assessment Scoring Rubric	
Score	**Description**
2	Clear and reasonable response that is supported by text evidence
1	Reasonable but vague response that is somewhat connected to text evidence
0	Does not respond to the question

Evidence may be specific words from the text or a paraphrase.

Mid-Unit Assessment

The Mid-Unit Assessment presents a snapshot of children's understanding at the key 3-week instructional interval. This test features two "cold read" reading selections and 10 selected response items—seven items on the featured comprehension skills in Weeks 1–3 and three items that ask children to show how context helps them identify the meaning of a vocabulary word.

Administering Mid-Unit Assessment

Each test should be administered at the end of Week 3 instruction. Make a copy of the assessment and the Scoring Sheet for each child.

After each child has a copy of the assessment, provide a version of the following directions: **Say:** *Write your name and the date on the question pages for this assessment.* (When children are finished, continue with the directions.) *You will read two selections and answer questions about them. Read the selections and the questions that follow them carefully. Choose the correct answer to each question and completely fill in the bubble next to it. When you have completed the assessment, put your pencil down and turn the pages over. You may begin now.*

NOTE: The directions above can be used when children take the Unit and Exit Assessments.

Evaluating the Mid-Unit Assessment

Each Mid-Unit Assessment is worth 10 points, with each item worth 1 point. An Answer Key is provided to help with scoring. Note success or difficulty with specific skills. Use this data to determine the instructional focus going forward. Reteach tested skills for children who score 5 points or less on the comprehension items and 2 points or less on the vocabulary items.

Unit and Exit Assessment

The Unit Assessment tests mastery of the key instructional content featured in the unit. This test features two "cold read" reading selections (one narrative text and one informational text) and 15 selected response items—ten items on the unit's comprehension skills and five items that ask children to show how context helps them identify the meaning of a vocabulary word.

The Exit Assessment is a "parallel" test to the Unit Assessment. It assesses the same skills and pool of vocabulary words using the same format. The key differentiator between the tests is the higher level of text complexity featured in the reading selections, a level more in line with the rigor found in Approaching Level *McGraw-Hill Reading Wonders* materials.

Moving from Unit to Exit Assessment

Administer the Unit Assessment to ALL children at the close of unit instruction. Make a copy of the assessment and the Scoring Sheet for each child. Each Unit Assessment is worth 15 points, with each item worth 1 point. An Answer Key is provided to help with scoring.

If children score 13 or higher on the Unit Assessment, administer the Exit Assessment. The Exit Assessment is ONLY for those children who reach this Unit Assessment benchmark.

Oral Reading Fluency Assessment

Fluency passages are included to help assess the level at which children have progressed beyond decoding into comprehension. When readers can read the words in connected text automatically, they are free to focus on using the critical thinking skills essential to constructing meaning from complex text.

24 fiction and nonfiction passages are included to help you assess fluency. The passages are set in three Unit/Lexile bands—the first set of eight is for Units 1 and 2, the next set of eight is for Units 3 and 4, and the final set of eight is for Units 5 and 6.

See pages 6 and 7 of *Fluency Assessment* for directions on administering and scoring oral reading fluency passages and for the unit-specific benchmark WCPM scores.

Transitioning into *McGraw-Hill Reading Wonders* Instruction

Moving children into Approaching Level *McGraw-Hill Reading Wonders* instruction at the completion of a unit should be guided by assessment data, performance during the unit instruction, and informal observation of children's progress.

Use the following assessment criteria to help judge readiness for Approaching Level designation and materials:

- Unit Assessment score of 13 or higher
- Ability to comprehend and analyze the Level Up Approaching Leveled Reader
- Score of 3 or higher on Level Up Write About Reading assignment
- Mastery of the unit benchmark skills in the Foundational Skills Kit and *Reading Wonders* Adaptive Learning
- WCPM score and accuracy rate that meet or exceed the unit goals
- Exit Assessment score of 13 or higher

Weekly
Assessment

Name: _____ Date: _____

Read "Get Well, Sam!" before you answer Numbers 1 through 5.

Get Well, Sam!

One day Sam the snake is sick.

Fred the frog visits Sam.

Sam is happy to see Fred.

Fred is Sam's friend.

Fred has an idea.

He can make a card for Sam!

All the animals write on the card.

Fred takes the card to Sam.

Sam feels happy!

Sam can always **depend** on Fred.

If Sam needs him, Fred is there.

Sam feels great the next day.

He is **perfectly** well!

Sam visits Fred.

He thanks Fred for the card.

GO ON →

Name: _____ Date: _____

Use "Get Well, Sam!" to answer Numbers 1 through 5.

1 Why does Fred visit Sam?

Circle the words that tell you.

2 What can Fred make for Sam?

Circle the words that tell you.

3 Why can Sam always *depend* on Fred?

Underline the sentence that tells you.

4 What is another way to say *perfectly* well?

Draw a box around your answer.

5 What does Sam do at the END of the story?

Circle the sentence that tells you.

STOP

Read "Rick's Trip" before you answer Numbers I through 5.

Rick's Trip

Rick gets a letter.

The letter is from Gran.

Gran lives in Italy.

Rick wants to visit Gran.

Mom and Rick fly on a plane.

Then they ride a train to Gran's house.

Rick hears people talk.

They speak a different **language**.

They use words Rick does not know.

Rick and Mom visit for a **week**.

Rick learns about Italy's **culture**.

He tries new food.

Gran shows him art.

Then they say goodbye to Gran.

It is time to fly home.

GO ON →

Name: _____ Date: _____

Use "Rick's Trip" to answer Numbers I through 5.

1 Where does Gran live?

_____

2 How do Rick and Mom get to Gran's house?

Draw a box around the sentences that tell.

3 Rick does not understand the words he hears.

2nd   U1 W2
         U1 W3
3 copies   ou why.

4   the *culture?*

3rd   t tell you.
4 copies   U1 W2
           U1 W3
5   visit Gran?

                           wer.

STOP

Read "The Lost Cat" before you answer Numbers 1 through 5.

The Lost Cat

Jen and Mom go to the park.

They have a picnic.

Jen sees a cat.

The cat looks lost.

Mom calls to the cat.

The cat looks hard at Mom.

The cat **stares** at Jen, too.

Jen puts milk in a bowl.

She puts the bowl down.

The cat drinks.

Jen asks, "Can we keep him?"

Mom says it is **proper**, or right, to take him home.

Mom reads the tag on the cat's collar.

Her name is Pip.

Pip lives near the park.

Jen and Mom take Pip home.

Now Jen wants a cat!

GO ON →

Name: _____ **Date:** _____

Use "The Lost Cat" to answer Numbers I through 5.

1 Where do Jen and Mom have a picnic?

Draw a box around the words that tell you.

2 What does *stares* mean?

Underline the words that give you a clue.

3 What does the cat drink?

_____

4 What word means the SAME as *proper*?

Underline the word in the story.

5 What does Jen want at the END of the story?

Draw a box around the answer.

STOP

Name: _____ Date: _____

Read "Mike and the Apes" before you answer Numbers I through 5.

Mike and the Apes

Mike works at the zoo.

He takes **care** of five apes.

He looks after them.

The apes **roam** around a big field.

They walk as much as they want.

They like to swing from ropes.

Mike makes sure the ropes are strong.

This keeps the apes safe.

Mike feeds the apes lots of plants.

He gives them water to drink.

Mike cleans the Ape House.

That is where the apes live.

Kids like to visit the zoo.

Mike tells them about the apes.

Mike likes his job.

GO ON →

Name: _____ Date: _____

Use "Mike and the Apes" to answer Numbers 1 through 5.

1 Where does Mike work?

Draw a box around the words that tell you.

2 What does *care* mean?

Underline the words that give you a clue.

3 What does *roam* mean?

Circle the word that gives you a clue.

4 What do apes eat?

Draw a box around the words that tell you.

5 Who likes to visit the zoo?

_____

STOP

Name: _____ **Date:** _____

Read "Food in the Family" before you answer Numbers 1 through 5.

Food in the Family

Mel and Em are sisters.

They grew up on a farm.

Their dad grows corn.

It is hard work.

The family has a shop, too.

Everyone has **jobs** at the shop.

Mom makes the food.

She makes pies with fresh fruit.

Mom taught the girls how to bake pies.

Em and Mel grew up. They moved to the city.

They baked pies at home.

Now the girls have a pie store.

They sell fresh fruit pies.

They sell pies to people in the store.

Customers love to buy their pies.

Mom and Dad are proud of Em and Mel.

GO ON →

Name: _____ Date: _____

Use "Food in the Family" to answer Numbers 1 through 5.

1 What does Dad grow?

_____

2 **Underline** the *jobs* Mom does at the shop.

3 Who taught Mel and Em how to bake pies?

Draw a box around the answer.

4 What do the sisters have now?

Draw a box around the answer.

5 Who are *customers*?

Underline the words that tell you.

STOP

Name: _____ Date: _____

Read "A Class Trip" before you answer Numbers 1 through 5.

A Class Trip

Tim has a class trip. His class visits a pond.

Beavers live in the pond. The class looks for them.

They see a tree stump. It has marks from teeth.

"A beaver chewed it," the teacher says.

Beavers **adapt**, or adjust, to their environment. Beavers have long teeth. Their teeth do not stop growing. Their teeth can chop wood. They use wood to build homes.

The class sees a pile of logs. It is in the middle of the pond. It is a beaver's house!

Two beavers swim by. They have wide, flat tails. The tails help them swim. This is an adaptation, too.

The class leaves the pond. Tim feels **eager** to go back to school. He looks forward to writing a report about beavers!

GO ON →

Name: _____ **Date:** _____

Use "A Class Trip" to answer Numbers 1 through 5.

1 Where does Tim's class go for their class trip?

  Draw a box around the sentence that tells you.

2 **Underline** the word that means the SAME as *adapt*.

3 What can beavers do with their teeth?

  Draw a box around your answer.

4 What does *eager* mean?

  Underline the words that give you a clue.

5 What does Tim want to do after the trip?

  _____

STOP

Name: _____ Date: _____

**Read "Bear and Turtle" before you answer
Numbers I through 5.**

Bear and Turtle

Bear sat on a rock. He was eating berries. Bear
wanted a friend to visit him.

Turtle walked by Bear. Turtle had lots of food.

Bear asked Turtle to talk to him. But Turtle was too
busy. Turtle was worried about winter. He did not
think he had enough food.

Turtle said it would snow soon. Bear did not
believe him. He did not think Turtle was telling
the truth.

That night there was a snow storm. Snow covered
the trees and rocks. Bear could not find food. He
looked near his cave. He looked all over the woods.
He could not find any food.

Turtle knew that Bear had no food. He gave Bear
some food to eat. Bear thanked Turtle.

Bear learned something important. The **lesson** was
that he must prepare for winter.

GO ON →

Name: _____ **Date:** _____

Use "Bear and Turtle" to answer Numbers 1 through 5.

1 What problem does Bear have AFTER the snow storm?

Draw a box around the sentence that tells you.

2 What does *believe* mean?

Underline the words that give you a clue.

3 What steps does Bear take to solve his problem?

Draw a box around the sentence that tells you.

4 How does Turtle help solve Bear's problem?

_____

5 What *lesson* does Bear learn?

Underline the words that tell you.

STOP

Name: _____ Date: _____

Read "Life in a Bay" before you answer Numbers I through 5.

Life in a Bay

I live near a bay. A bay forms where a river meets the sea. Salt water and fresh water mix.

I stop at the bay after school. Today I see lots of plants. Bay soil is good for plants. The plants' roots are **buried**, or covered, by mud.

A Good Place for Animals

I also see lots of different animals. Many animals live in this **habitat**. It is a place where animals can survive. Some animals come from rivers. Others come from the sea.

I see many fish today. Small fish like the calm water. Larger salmon also lay eggs here. The eggs stay safe. Then they move to the sea.

Some birds eat the plants in a bay. Others eat the fish. I see herons standing in the water. They are hunting fish. I could stay here all day!

GO ON →

Use "Life in a Bay" to answer Numbers I through 5.

1 What is this article about?

_____

2 **Underline** the word that means the SAME as *buried.*

3 What does *habitat mean*?

Underline the words that give you a clue.

4 What do small fish like about a bay?

Draw a box around the words that tell you.

5 **Draw a box** around the words that tell you what herons eat in the bay.

STOP

Name: _____ Date: _____

Read "Zebras" before you answer Numbers I through 5.

Zebras

Zebras live in Africa. They live in the wild. Their **offspring,** or children, are called foals. Zebras look a lot like horses.

A mother zebra is an **adult**. It is fully grown. It has one foal. The mother keeps other zebras away from her foal. The foal learns who its mother is.

A foal stays with its mother. The mother shows the foal how to find food. Zebras eat grasses.

Zebras have stripes. The stripes are black and white. Foals have stripes, too. But their stripes are not black and white. Stripes help zebras hide. They hide in the tall grass.

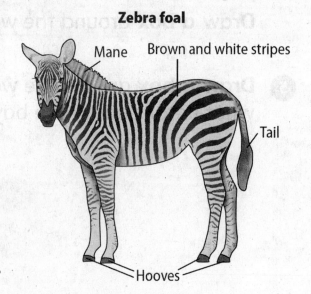

Zebra foal
Mane   Brown and white stripes
Tail
Hooves

A foal grows up in a few years. Then it is an **adult** zebra.

GO ON →

Use "Zebras" to answer Numbers 1 through 5.

1 What is this article about?

_____

2 **Underline** the word that means about the SAME as *offspring*.

3 **Underline** the clues that help you know what *adult* means.

4 What do zebras eat?

Draw a box around the word that tells you.

5 Look at the diagram. What are a zebra's feet called?

Circle the label that tells you.

STOP

Read the poem "Pat's Puppy" before you answer Numbers I through 5.

Pat's Puppy

One fine day Pat got a pet.

It was his very best gift yet.

She was a puppy, small and sweet,

With soft brown fur and tiny feet.

Pat heard his pup's unhappy cries,

He saw her deep and sad brown eyes.

But when she saw Pat's friendly face,

Her little tail began to race.

Pat smiled, and then he picked her up,

Which made her quite a happy pup!

GO ON →

Name: _____ Date: _____

Use "Pat's Puppy" to answer Numbers 1 through 5.

1 What color is Pat's puppy?

Draw a box around the word that tells you.

2 **Underline** the word that rhymes with "eyes."

3 **Circle** the words that tell you what Pat's puppy saw.

4 "Her little tail began to race." How many beats are in this line?

_____

5 What does Pat do to make his puppy happy?

_____

STOP

Name: _____ Date: _____

Read "This Is Friction!" before you answer Numbers 1 through 5.

This Is Friction!

You kick a ball. How far will it roll? When will it stop? It depends. If it lands on rough grass, it will stop soon. If it lands on a smooth playground, it will keep rolling.

Friction will stop the ball. Friction is a **force**. A force is a push or a pull.

Friction happens when two **objects**, or things, rub together. Rough surfaces have more friction than smooth surfaces. Sand is rough. Ice is smooth. Sand has more friction than ice. It is hard to push a sled on sand. It is easy to push a sled on ice.

Why is it easy to slip on a wet floor? Water makes the floor very smooth. There is not much friction.

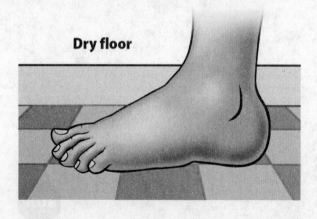

Dry floor

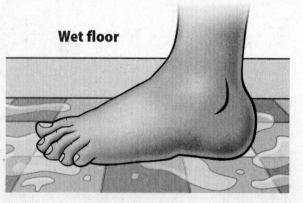

Wet floor

GO ON →

Name: _____ Date: _____

Use "This Is Friction!" to answer Numbers 1 through 5.

1 You kick a ball. What stops the ball?

_____

2 **Underline** the sentence that explains what *force* means.

3 **Circle** the word that means the SAME as *objects*.

4 What does the author want you to know about rough and smooth surfaces?

Draw a box around the sentence that tells you.

5 Look back at the text and the diagram. What is the author's purpose for writing this selection?

_____

_____

STOP

Name: _____ **Date:** _____

Read "The Rainbow" before you answer Numbers 1 through 5.

The Rainbow

Bob and Dave were in their cabin at camp getting ready for their first soccer match. Suddenly the boys heard a crack of thunder. They ran to the cabin window.

"I don't like this," Bob **grumbled**. He sounded unhappy.

"It will stop soon," Dave said. "Then we can play."

The rain did not stop. The boys ran outside at game time. But they knew the match would be called off. The soccer field was filled with mud.

Then the boys walked slowly back to their cabin. As they walked, the rain stopped. Dave saw a huge rainbow in the sky.

"Look up!" Dave said. "It's amazing!"

Pleased and **delighted**, they observed a bright rainbow. The boys were able to see every band of color. Then they raced each other back to the cabin.

GO ON →

Name: _____ **Date:** _____

Use "Rainbow" to answer Numbers I through 5.

1 Where are Bob and Dave in the BEGINNING of the story?

Draw a box around the words that tell you.

2 Underline the words that help you understand what *grumbled* means.

3 The boys see the field filled with mud.

Draw a box around the words that tell you. what they do next.

4 Why does Dave tell Bob to look up?

_____

5 Underline the word that means about the SAME as *delighted*.

STOP

Name: _____ Date: _____

Read "Community Gardens" before you answer
Numbers I through 5.

Community Gardens

Cara and Leo help start community gardens. They
hold meetings for people who want to help. Cara
and Leo listen to people's **ideas**. Then, they share
their thoughts. Gardens make a city look nice. They
help bring people together.

One problem is finding a place for the garden. A
solution is to use land owned by the city. When
they solve the problem, work begins. People
volunteer to help. They start by clearing the land.
They pull weeds and remove trash. This is good
exercise. They learn how to grow food. They meet
new people.

Some people want to plant fruits and vegetables.
People save money when they grow their own food.
They also learn how to eat better. Extra food can
be sold at the farmers' market. The money helps
the community. It helps Cara and Leo start more
gardens. Community gardens make a city better!

GO ON →

Name: _____ Date: _____

**Use "Community Gardens" to answer Numbers I
through 5.**

1 What do Cara and Leo help start?

Draw a box around the words that tell you.

2 What does *ideas* mean?

Underline the word that gives you a clue.

3 What does *solution* mean?

Underline the words that give you a clue.

4 What do people learn when they grow their
own food?

Draw a box around the words that tell you.

5 What is the author's purpose for writing
"Community Gardens"?

_____

_____

STOP

Name: _____ Date: _____

Read "Blizzards" before you answer Numbers
1 through 5.

Blizzards

Winter weather can cause problems. Schools and
businesses may have to close. Snow may block
the roads.

More Than a Snowstorm

A blizzard is a big snowstorm with **harsh**, or rough,
winds. A lot of snow falls in a short time. A blizzard
can be **dangerous**, or cause harm. Trees can fall.
Power lines can be knocked down.

The Northeastern United States is known for
blizzards. They are called "Nor'easters." They can
last for more than a day.

Be Prepared!

How can you stay safe during a blizzard? First,
listen to the news. If you hear a blizzard is coming,
be ready. Buy canned food and bottled water. Get
a first-aid kit. Make sure your flashlights work. Then
stay inside. It is easier to stay safe when you are
prepared!

GO ON →

Name: _____ **Date:** _____

Use "Blizzards" to answer Numbers 1 through 5.

1 What is this article mainly about?

_____

2 **Underline** the word that means about the SAME as *harsh*.

3 What does *dangerous* mean?

Circle the words that give you a clue.

4 How long can a "Nor'easter" last?

Draw a box around the words that tell you.

5 What is easier to do when you are prepared?

Draw a box around the words that tell you.

Name: _____ **Date:** _____

Read "The Dance Teacher" before you answer Numbers I through 5.

The Dance Teacher

Marcia Dale Weary is a dancer. She also is a teacher. In 1955 she opened a ballet school. She likes to teach children. She teaches them to express themselves.

The students learn how to move to **music**. They listen to the sounds made by instruments. They express themselves by dancing.

Some students are only three years old. As students learn, they begin to **understand**, or know, the basics of ballet. They learn how to balance. They learn how to spin and jump.

Marcia thinks children who dance understand how to work hard. "They have a goal they want to reach," she says. "They want to dance. It makes me happy."

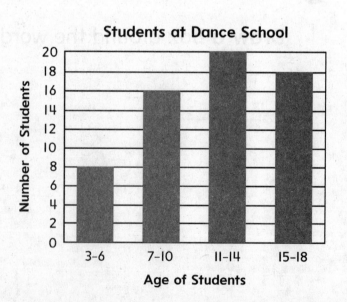

Students at Dance School

GO ON →

Name: _____ **Date:** _____

Use "The Dance Teacher" to answer Numbers 1 through 5.

1 What did Marcia Dale Weary do in 1955?

Draw a box around the answer.

2 **Underline** the words that tell you what *music* means.

3 Look at the graph. How many students at the school are 7–10 years old?

Circle the answer on the graph.

4 **Underline** the word that means about the SAME as *understand*.

5 What is the MAIN idea of the article?

_____

STOP

Name: _____ Date: _____

Read "Niagara Falls" before you answer
Numbers 1 through 5.

Niagara Falls

Waterfalls are powerful. Water drops from very
high. It lands in a river below.

Three Waterfalls, Two Places

Niagara Falls is located where New York meets
Canada. Three beautiful waterfalls are there.

The biggest waterfall is in Canada. Water drops
down more than 100 feet. It is called Horseshoe
Falls because of its shape. It curves around like the
letter *U*. Bridal Veil Falls is the smallest waterfall. It
is on the New York side. So is American Falls.

Seasons at the Falls

The **seasons** change a lot at Niagara Falls. It is
very cold in winter. There are few visitors. But in
summer, the weather is more **temperate**. It is not
too hot or too cold. Summer is when most people
visit. They can ride a boat and walk through a cave
to see the falls. They get splashed by the water.
That's part of the fun!

GO ON →

Name: _____ **Date:** _____

Use "Niagara Falls" to answer Numbers 1 through 5.

1 How is Bridal Veil Falls DIFFERENT from Horseshoe falls?

Circle the sentence that tells you.

2 Which heading helps you find out where Niagara Falls is located?

Circle the heading.

3 How are Bridal Veil Falls and American Falls ALIKE?

Write your answer.

_____

4 **Underline** the names of two *seasons* that are being compared.

5 **Draw a box** around the sentence that tells you what *temperate* means.

STOP

Name: _____ Date: _____

Read "Forest Fires" before you answer Numbers 1 through 5.

Forest Fires

Forest fires are wild fires in wooded areas. **Active**, or lively, forest fires move fast. They can destroy thousands of acres.

What Causes Forest Fires?

Fires need fuel, oxygen, and heat. In a forest, the trees are the fuel. Oxygen is in the air. All that's missing is the heat. Lightning can strike a tree in the forest. As a result, a forest fire starts. Half of all forest fires are caused by lightning. People cause the other half.

Effects of Forest Fires

Forest fires have negative effects. Raging fires can destroy anything **solid**, or firm, in their path. Forest fires create smog. They harm animals.

Forest fires also have positive effects. They get rid of diseased plants. They kill harmful insects. Fires can destroy tall trees. This lets more sunlight reach the forest floor. Different seeds are able to grow.

GO ON →

Use "Forest Fires" to answer Numbers 1 through 5.

1 **Underline** the word that means about the SAME as *active.*

2 What happens as a result of lightning striking a tree in the forest?

Draw a box around the effect.

3 What does *solid* mean?

Underline the word that gives you a clue.

4 Which section of the article explains the results of forest fires?

Circle the heading.

5 What can happen when more sunlight reaches the forest floor?

Write your answer.

_____

STOP

Name: _____ Date: _____

Read "Living in Lima" before you answer Numbers 1 through 5.

Living in Lima

My name is Pablo. I live in Lima with my family. Lima is the capital city of Peru. Peru is in South America. I speak Spanish.

My friend, Claire, just moved to Lima with her family. They moved from the United States. Claire speaks English. I am helping Claire learn Spanish. I know many more Spanish words than she does.

Claire and I like to **travel,** or go from one place to another, on our bikes. We like to ride around our neighborhood. Claire points at things, and I tell her the Spanish word for each thing. Later, Claire writes the words down. Then I check her spelling.

Claire and I like to eat lunch together in the park. She brings tomato salad. I bring potatoes filled with beef. We want our lunches to be alike, so we share our food. Then we buy ice cream. In Peru, ice cream is called *helado*. Ice cream is our **favorite** dessert. We like it better than anything!

GO ON →

Name: _____ Date: _____

Use "Living in Lima" to answer Numbers 1 through 5.

1 Pablo and Claire are from DIFFERENT places.

Draw a box around where Claire comes from.

2 **Underline** the words that mean about the SAME as *travel*.

3 Why is Pablo helping Claire learn Spanish?

Write the answer.

_____

_____

4 **Draw a box** around what Claire and Pablo do to make their lunches ALIKE.

5 Claire and Pablo buy ice cream because it is their *favorite* dessert.

Underline the sentence that tells you what *favorite* means.

STOP

Name: _____ Date: _____

**Read "Ant and Eagle" before you answer
Numbers I through 5.**

Ant and Eagle

Narrator: One fine day, Ant was by the river.

Ant: I am thirsty!

(Ant tries to drink from the river and falls in.)

Ant: Help! I cannot swim!

(Ant yelled out again. Eagle hears Ant **holler**. She
flies down and pulls Ant from the water. Eagle
always helps a friend in need.)

Ant: Thank you, Eagle!

Eagle: You are welcome!

(Eagle flies away.)

Narrator: Later that day, Ant was in the forest.
He saw Bird Catcher sneak up behind Eagle.

Ant: Eagle helped me before. Now it is my turn.
I will **dash** over and help her.

(Ant runs over and tickles Bird Catcher's leg. Bird
Catcher looks down, and Eagle flies away.)

Narrator: Ant and Eagle helped each other that
day. They have been friends ever since.

GO ON →

Name: _____ **Date:** _____

Use "Ant and Eagle" to answer Numbers 1 through 5.

1 What does *holler* mean?

Underline the words that give you a clue.

2 **Draw a box** around the sentence that tells how Eagle helps Ant.

3 Why does Ant help Eagle?

Draw a box around the answer.

4 What does *dash* mean?

Underline the words that give you a clue.

5 What is the lesson you learn from the story?

Write your answer.

_____

STOP

Name: _____ Date: _____

Read "Where I Like to Be" before you answer Numbers 1 through 5.

Where I Like to Be

One day as I sat by a tree,

The wind blew through the branches.

It made a little song for me,

which was as sweet as honey.

One day as I sat by the sea,

The sea sang a special song.

The sea knew where I like to be.

And it played it's sweet song for me.

One day as I sat under the sun.

I sang some special songs

Then the sun had to leave. So did I.

But I will be back tomorrow.

There's always something fun to do

When I spend the day outside!

GO ON →

Name: _____ Date: _____

Use "Where I Like to Be" to answer Numbers I through 5.

1 In the first stanza, where does the narrator like to be?

Draw a box around the words that tell you.

2 What phrase does the poet repeat three times?

Write the phrase.

_____

3 **Draw a box** around a word in each stanza that gives you a clue about where the poem takes place.

4 Find the line in the third stanza where four words start with the same sound.

Circle the words.

5 **Draw a box** around the lines that tell you the theme of the poem.

STOP

Weekly Assessment · Unit 4, Week 5   Grade 2   **49**

Name: _____ **Date:** _____

Read "Saturday" before you answer Numbers 1 through 5.

Saturday

I was glad it was Saturday. All week I had been making a list of outdoor activities I wanted to do.

"This is my day," I said to myself. "I am definitely going to do everything on this list. That's a **promise**!"

As I was heading outside, I saw my neighbor, Ms. Beal. She wore a big, heavy cast on her leg.

"Silas, I'm having some **issues**," said Ms. Beal.

"What problems are you having?" I asked.

"I need to clean out my basement. But I can't get up and down the steps. Can you help me?"

This sounded like a tough job that could take a long time. What about all my plans? Then I remembered my mom. She always helped our neighbors, no matter what else she had to do.

I spent the rest of the morning cleaning out Ms. Beal's basement. It was hard work. When I was finished, though, I felt great! My list of activities did not seem so important after all.

GO ON →

Weekly Assessment · Unit 5, Week 1

Use "Saturday" to answer Numbers 1 through 5.

1 What is Silas's point of view at the BEGINNING of the story?

Write the answer.

_____

2 What *promise* does Silas make?

Underline the sentence that tells you.

3 What is another word for *issues*?

Underline the word that tells you.

4 What is Silas's point of view AFTER Ms. Beal asks him to help her?

Draw a box around the words that tell you.

5 What is Silas' point of view at the END of the story?

Draw a box around the words that tell you.

STOP

Name: _____ **Date:** _____

Read "The Class Play" before you answer Numbers I through 5.

The Class Play

Ed and Amanda talk about "Beauty and the Beast" at lunch. It is the new class play. Their class will perform the play next month.

Amanda wants to make the costumes. She thinks sewing will be a **peaceful**, quiet job.

Ed has been in plays before. He wants to try out for the Beast. "I'm the best actor in our class," he tells Amanda. "I should get that part."

Ed doesn't get the part. "I don't care about this play," he says.

"You can do other things," Amanda says. "You like art. Why don't you paint the scenery?" Ed is not sure.

Ed takes her advice. He paints the scenery with some other students. They all **cooperate**, or work together, to finish the job. Ed paints a huge castle and a forest. His classmates clap when they see it.

"Thanks for the great idea," he tells Amanda. "This play was a lot of fun."

GO ON →

Name: _____   Date: _____

Use "The Class Play" to answer Numbers I through 5.

1 **Underline** the word with the SAME meaning as *peaceful.*

2 What is Ed's point of view about who should play the part of the Beast?

   Draw a box around the words that tell you.

3 What is Ed's point of view about the play?

   Draw a box around the words that tell you.

4 What does *cooperate* mean?

   Underline the words that give you a clue.

5 How can you tell that Ed's point of view has changed about the play at the END of the story?

   Write your answer.

_____

STOP

Read "Sandra Day O'Connor" before you answer Numbers I through 5.

Sandra Day O'Connor

Sandra Day O'Connor was the first woman to be a judge on the Supreme Court. The Supreme Court is the highest court in the United States.

Sandra grew up in Arizona. She went to college in California. After college, Sandra wanted to be a lawyer. First, she went to law school to **study**. She learned many things about the law. Then, Sandra went back to Arizona.

Next, Sandra wanted to get a job in a law firm. But no one would hire a woman lawyer. So she started her own law firm. Others did not think the business would **succeed**, but it did very well!

Sandra was smart and worked very hard. She is a hero for many people!

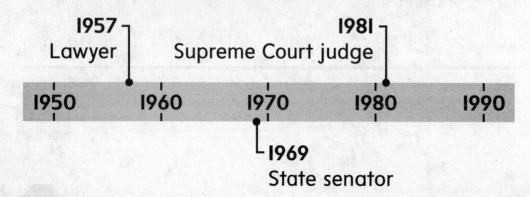

GO ON →

Use "Sandra Day O'Connor" to answer Numbers I through 5.

1 What was the FIRST thing Sandra did after college to become a lawyer?

Draw a box around the words that tell you.

2 **Underline** the sentence that tells you what *study* means.

3 What did Sandra want to do AFTER she went back to Arizona?

Write the answer.

_____

4 What does *succeed* mean?

Underline the words that tell you.

5 In what year did Sandra become a Supreme Court judge?

Circle your answer on the time line.

STOP

Name: _____ Date: _____

Read "Play Ball!" before you answer Numbers 1 through 5.

Play Ball!

The twins raced home with the terrible news, carrying their new ball, bat, and gloves.

"Dad!" Jenna called as she ran up the driveway. "Our baseball field has disappeared!"

Their father was **curious** and wanted to learn more. "What do you mean it disappeared?"

"Well, the field is there," Jason explained. "But garbage is everywhere, and it is too dirty to use!"

"You two **rarely** run out of ideas," Dad said. "That doesn't happen often. What can we do?"

Jenna and Jason thought for a few minutes. "Why don't we work together to clean it up?"

Dad thought that was an excellent suggestion. On Saturday, the twins and their friends gathered at the baseball field. They picked up bottles and collected metal cans and paper.

"I'll take this to the community center where it can be recycled to save resources," Dad told them.

"Let's play ball!" Jason shouted happily.

GO ON →

Name: _____ Date: _____

Use "Play Ball!" to answer Numbers I through 5.

1 How does Jenna describe the twins' problem?

Draw a box around Jenna's words.

2 What words have about the SAME meaning
as *curious*?

Underline the words.

3 **Underline** the words that help you understand
what *rarely* means.

4 How do the twins solve their problem?

Write your answer.

_____

_____

5 What clue shows you that the problem has
been solved?

Draw a box around the text that tells you.

STOP

Read "The Big Bee" before you answer Numbers I through 5.

The Big Bee

There is a big spelling contest every year. It is the National Spelling Bee. Lots of kids enter the big bee. Only one can win.

The bee has many **rules**. They tell what is allowed. Kids have to follow the rules. If they do not, they cannot be in the contest.

One rule is that kids must be in Grade 8 or below. Here is another rule. Kids have to win local spelling bees before they can be in the big bee.

Early in the bee, each word is worth one point. Later, each word is worth three points. The kids with the most points are the best spellers.

Finally, after a few days, the 50 best spellers meet. The one who spells the most words right wins the big bee. It pays to be a good speller. One year, the winner got $30,000!

If you...	Then you...
Are in Grade 9	Cannot enter
Spell a word wrong	Cannot win

GO ON →

Name: _____ **Date:** _____

Use "The Big Bee" to answer Numbers I through 5.

1 What are *rules*?

Underline the words that give you a clue.

2 What happens if kids do NOT follow the rules of the National Spelling Bee?

Draw a box around the effect.

3 **Underline** the words that give you a clue about what *finally* means in this article.

4 What causes someone to win the big bee?

Write the answer.

_____

_____

5 Look at the chart. What is the effect of spelling a word wrong?

Circle the answer in the chart.

STOP

Read "Why a Fawn Has Spots" before you answer Numbers 1 through 5.

Why a Fawn Has Spots

Long ago, Animal King gave gifts to animals. The gifts helped the animals survive. Birds got wings. Deer got speed. Cats got claws. Then Animal King rested.

One day a deer brought her fawn to see Animal King. "Sir, I run very fast because of your gift," she said. "But my young son has no gift. He is not fast."

Animal King thought hard. He touched the fawn's fur. Many white spots **appeared,** or came into sight. The king told the fawn the spots would fade as he grew older.

"What will this gift do?" the fawn wondered.

Later, the deer and her fawn heard wolves. The deer ran away. The fawn hid in the bushes. The wolves ran right past him!

Now the fawn understood his gift. "Because I am young and cannot run fast, my spots protect me by helping me hide. When I **develop** and grow to become a deer, I will be able to run fast and protect myself."

GO ON →

Name: _____ **Date:** _____

Use "Why a Fawn Has Spots" to answer
Numbers 1 through 5.

1 How do Animal King's gifts help animals?

Draw a box around the answer.

2 What does *appeared* mean?

Underline the words that tell you.

3 How does the fawn's gift help him when the
wolves come?

Draw a box around the sentence that
tells you.

4 **Underline** the clue that helps you understand
what *develop* means.

5 What is the lesson you learn from the story?

Write your answer.

_____

STOP

Read "Trash or Treasure?" before you answer
Numbers 1 through 5.

Trash or Treasure?

We use energy when we turn on a light or work
on a computer. Where does energy come from?

Energy from the Earth

It comes from fuels like coal, oil, and natural
gas. These resources are found **underground,** or
beneath the surface of the earth. They will run out
someday.

How can we make sure we will have enough
power in the future? Power is the energy that
makes lights and machines work. We must find
resources that will not run out.

Energy from Trash

In 2010, the U.S. produced 250 million tons of
trash! When trash is in a landfill, it produces a gas.
This gas is mostly methane. It is the main
ingredient in natural gas. Methane is captured at
plants. Then it is burned and used to make energy.
Trash is a renewable source of energy. We will
never run out of trash!

GO ON →

Name: _____ **Date:** _____

Use "Trash or Treasure?" to answer Numbers I through 5.

1 What are some things we use energy for?

   Draw a box around the answer.

2 **Underline** the words that tell you what *underground* means.

3 What does *power* mean?

   Underline the words that give you a clue.

4 Where does the author explain how trash is turned into energy?

   Circle the heading of the section.

5 What is the author's purpose for writing this article?

   Write your answer.

   _____

   _____

Name: _____ Date: _____

Read "Underground Astronauts" before you answer Numbers I through 5.

Underground Astronauts

Astronauts need to help each other when they are in space. They train together to learn how to work as a team.

A group in Europe **prepares** astronauts to work as a team in space. To help them get ready, the group sends astronauts to a cave in Italy. They stay there for a week. The astronauts work together in extreme conditions. They study rocks and animals. They explore together.

In 2012, a team saw strange creatures near a pond in the cave. They were like small shellfish. One team member set bait near the pond. Another team member caught some of the creatures. The team saved them and brought them outside. Other team members studied them. The team learned that they had discovered a new animal!

As a **result** of, or because of, this training, the astronauts on the team will be ready for their next mission to space! They will need to work together!

GO ON →

Use "Underground Astronauts" to answer Numbers 1 through 5.

1 What does *prepares* mean?

Circle the words that give you a clue.

2 Did the astronauts work alone or together in the cave?

Draw a box around the sentence that tells you.

3 What did the astronauts discover?

Draw a box around the text that tells you.

4 Circle the words that help you understand the meaning of *result*.

5 What is the MAIN idea of this article?

Write your answer.

_____

STOP

Name: _____   Date: _____

Read "Pennies Make a Difference" before you answer Numbers 1 through 5.

Pennies Make a Difference

Some people think pennies are not useful. They think pennies do not have any **value**, or worth. But pennies can be important. Some groups collect pennies for different causes. This is a great **system** for putting pennies to use.

One program is called Pennies for Patients. Students collect pennies and other spare change to help sick kids. They learn the value of money. Schools across the country have raised millions of dollars. This kind of program helps schools, too. Schools that collect the most money win prizes.

Pennies are not a problem after all. They can help in a big way!

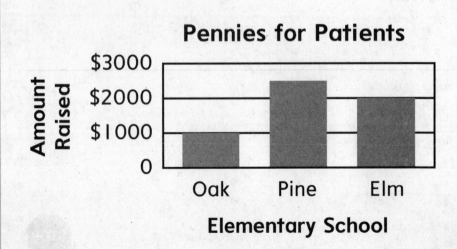

Pennies for Patients

GO ON →

Name: _____ Date: _____

Use "Pennies Make a Difference" to answer Numbers I through 5.

1 What problem do some people have with pennies?

Draw a box around the sentence that tells you.

2 **Circle** the word that means about the SAME as *value.*

3 What *system* do some groups have for using pennies?

Write your answer.

_____

4 How does Pennies for Patients use pennies?

Draw a box around the answer.

5 Look at the graph. How much money did Elm Elementary School raise for Pennies for Patients?

Underline your answer on the graph.

STOP

Name: _____ **Date:** _____

Read the poem "Off to the Stars, or Under the Sea" before you answer Numbers 1 through 5.

Off to the Stars, or Under the Sea

My dad brought home a cardboard box,

But that's not what I see.

I see a shiny rocket ship

Or a submarine under the sea.

I get inside my rocket ship

And blast off to the stars!

I make a stop to get moon rocks

On my way to amazing Mars.

Now my box is a submarine

That dives beneath the sea.

Look at the fun I can create

With just a plain cardboard box and me!

GO ON →

Name: _____ **Date:** _____

Use "Off to the Stars, or Under the Sea" to answer Numbers I through 5.

1 How many beats are in the first line of the poem?

   Write the number of beats.

_____

2 What is the speaker's point of view about the cardboard box?

   Draw a box around the line in the first verse that gives you a clue.

3 **Draw a box** around the word that shows the speaker's point of view about Mars.

4 **Underline** the two unlike things that are being compared in the last verse of the poem.

5 What is the speaker's point of view about the cardboard box in the last verse?

   Draw a box around the line that tells you.

STOP

Mid-Unit
Assessment

Read "Willy and Ollie" before you answer Numbers I through 5.

Willy and Ollie

Willy Whale lived on Sea Street.

Ollie Octopus lived next door.

One day, Willy found a new house.

"I have so much stuff," Willy wailed.

"How will I move?

I'm **afraid** it will take a week!"

"Don't be scared," Ollie said. "I'll help."

Ollie looked in Willie's house.

"Wow! You do have lots of stuff!"

"I know," Willy said. "How can you help?"

"I will use my eight arms!" Ollie said.

Ollie started grabbing things.

He helped Willy move all his stuff.

It took an hour.

"Thanks!" Willy said.

GO ON →

"Enjoy your new house," Ollie said. "Bye."

"Wait! Can I help you?" Willy cried.

Ollie thought for a moment.

"Yes," he said. "There is a big rock by my house.
It blocks my window.
I cannot see anything!"

"I will use my strong body!" Willy said.

The friends went to Ollie's house.
Willy pushed the rock.
He pushed hard.
The rock rolled away.

"Thanks!" Ollie said.

"Enjoy your view," Willy said. "Bye."

"Wait! Stay for dinner," Ollie cried.

"Thanks. I will," Willy said.

GO ON →

Name: _____ **Date:** _____

Use "Willy and Ollie" to answer Numbers 1 through 5.

1 Why is Willy worried at the BEGINNING?

Ⓐ He finds a new house.

Ⓑ He has too much stuff to move.

Ⓒ He needs to help Ollie move a rock.

2 Read these sentence from the story.

"I have so much stuff," Willy wailed.
"How will I move?
I'm *afraid* it will take a week!"
"Don't be scared," Ollie said.

Which word means about the SAME
as *afraid*?

Ⓐ scared

Ⓑ stuff

Ⓒ wailed

GO ON →

3 How long does it take to move Willy's stuff?

Ⓐ a moment

Ⓑ an hour

Ⓒ a week

4 How does Willy help Ollie?

Ⓐ Willy helps Ollie move.

Ⓑ Willy fixes Ollie dinner.

Ⓒ Willy moves the big rock.

5 Where do Willy and Ollie have dinner?

Ⓐ at Willy's new house

Ⓑ at Willy's old house

Ⓒ at Ollie's house

GO ON →

Read "Kay's New Bunny" before you answer Numbers 6 through 10.

Kay's New Bunny

Kay and Mom are at the park.

Kay watches the dogs play.

Kay starts to **plead**. "Mom, can I —"

"Don't beg," Mom says. "We talked about this.
We can't have a dog. We don't have a yard."

That night, Kay thinks hard. A dog needs a yard.
But some pets live indoors. Bunnies live indoors.
A bunny lives in a cage.

"Mom!" Kay cries. "Can I get a bunny? Please."

"Okay. We'll go to the animal shelter."

The next day, Mom drives Kay to the shelter.
A man shows them an area marked "Rabbits."

GO ON →

"I don't want a rabbit," Kay says.
"I want a bunny. Aren't they **different**?"

"No," the man says.
"Rabbits and bunnies are the same."

Kay watches a rabbit. He is in his cage.
He is cute. He is fuzzy.

"He needs a cage," the man says.
"A rabbit needs toys. He needs grass to eat.
He needs water."

"Can I get him, Mom?" Kay asks.
"I promise to take care of him."
Mom agrees.

That night, Kay is in her room.
She watches her new pet playing.
He is in his cage.

Mom comes in. "What did you name him?"

"I call him Bunny!"

GO ON ➔

Name: _____ Date: _____

Read "Kay's New Bunny" before you answer Numbers 6 through 10.

6 Read these sentences from the story.

> Kay starts to *plead*. "Mom, can I —"
> "Don't beg," Mom says.

Which word means about the SAME as *plead*?

Ⓐ beg

Ⓑ can

Ⓒ starts

7 Kay can't have a dog because

Ⓐ a dog lives in a cage.

Ⓑ she doesn't have a yard.

Ⓒ dogs cannot go to the park.

8 Where does Kay go to get a rabbit?

Ⓐ to the park

Ⓑ to her room

Ⓒ to the shelter

GO ON →

9 Read these sentences from the story.

"I don't want a rabbit," Kay says.
"I want a bunny. Aren't they *different*?"

"No," the man says.
"Rabbits and bunnies are the same."

Which word means almost the OPPOSITE
of *different*?

Ⓐ rabbit

Ⓑ same

Ⓒ want

10 How does Kay change from the BEGINNING to
the END?

Ⓐ At first she is sad and then she is happy.

Ⓑ At first she is happy and then she is sad.

Ⓒ At first she is helpful and then she is afraid.

STOP

Read "Sally the Snake" before you answer Numbers 1 through 5.

Sally the Snake

I like watching animals on the weekend. After breakfast, I head outside. I sit on my deck. My deck is beside a swamp. From my deck, I see Sally slide out of the water. She curls up on a rock. Sally is a snake. She lives near my house.

Sally's Home

Sally lives in the Everglades. The Everglades are an area in Florida. It is a very wet area. There are lakes. There are swamps. Many plants grow in the water.

The Everglades have a warm **climate**. There are two seasons. The weather during wet season is very hot. It rains a lot. The dry season is nice and warm. But there is less rain.

GO ON →

Lying in the Sun

Sally is **fond** of the warm weather. She likes the
hot sun. Like all snakes, she has cold blood. Her
body does not heat itself. To keep warm, she lies
in the sun. The sun heats her body. She looks like
she is asleep.

Time for Dinner

The sun sets. Night falls. Mom calls me to dinner. I
look out at Sally. She leaves her rock. She slides
into the water to eat. It's time for her dinner, too.

GO ON →

Use "Sally the Snake" to answer Numbers 1 through 5.

1 What is this article about?

Ⓐ the Everglades

Ⓑ the weather in the Everglades

Ⓒ a snake that lives in the Everglades

2 In the Everglades, many plants grow

Ⓐ on a rock.

Ⓑ on the deck.

Ⓒ in the water.

3 Read these sentences from the article.

> **The Everglades have a warm *climate*. There are two seasons. The weather during wet season is very hot. It rains a lot. The dry season is nice and warm. But there is less rain.**

Which word helps you figure out what *climate* means?

Ⓐ weather

Ⓑ nice

Ⓒ less

GO ON →

4 Read these sentences from the article.

**Sally is *fond* of the warm weather.
She likes the hot sun.**

Which word helps you figure out what
fond means?

Ⓐ warm

Ⓑ likes

Ⓒ sun

5 What do you learn about Sally under the
subhead **Lying in the Sun**?

Ⓐ Sally has warm blood.

Ⓑ Sally eats when the sun comes up.

Ⓒ Sally lies in the sun to warm her body.

GO ON →

Read "Taz Sees a Skunk" before you answer Numbers 6 through 10.

Taz Sees a Skunk

Jean gets up early. She **peeks** out her window. She looks in the back yard. This is a game she plays with Taz. Taz is Jean's dog. When Jean looks out, Taz runs to the window. Today, Jean does not see Taz.

"Oh, no," Jean says. "Taz is gone!"

Jean and her mom go outside. They look for Taz.

"Did you leave the gate open?" Mom asks.

"I must have," Jean said.

Jean looks down the street. She sees Taz. Taz is lying down. Taz is watching a bush.

"Taz," Jean calls out. Taz looks, but does not move.

A small, black animal comes out of the bush. It has a white stripe on its back. It has a long tail. Taz keeps watching.

GO ON →

"Is that a cat?" Jean asks.

"That is a skunk," Mom says. "Taz should be careful."

"Why is that, Mom?" Jean asks.

"Skunks have a liquid they spray," Mom said. "This helps keep them safe. It smells very bad. It smells like rotten eggs. The skunk will spray if it is in danger. A skunk can spray up to ten feet. Even a bear will run from skunk spray."

Mom and Jean watch. The skunk walks up to Taz. Taz lies very still. Soon, the skunk leaves.

"Wow, that was close," Jean says. "Come here, Taz!"

"You are a good dog," Mom says. "You stayed very calm. Jean, please make sure you shut the gate."

"I will, Mom," Jean says. "And you stay away from skunks, Taz. You do not want to get sprayed."

Taz barks. Mom and Jean laugh. They all walk home.

GO ON →

Name: _____ Date: _____

Use "Taz Sees a Skunk" to answer Numbers 6 through 10.

6 Read these sentences from the story.

Jean gets up early. She *peeks* out her window. She looks in the back yard.

Which word helps you figure out what *peeks* means?

Ⓐ early

Ⓑ window

Ⓒ looks

7 What is Jean's problem?

Ⓐ Her dog is gone.

Ⓑ She wakes up late.

Ⓒ She sees a skunk.

GO ON →

8 What step does Jean take to help solve her problem?

Ⓐ She calls her dad at work.

Ⓑ She asks her friends to look for the dog.

Ⓒ She goes with her mom to look for the dog.

9 Where happens in the MIDDLE of the story?

Ⓐ Taz watches a skunk in a bush.

Ⓑ Jean peeks out of her window.

Ⓒ Taz barks and Mom laughs.

10 What happens at the END of the story?

Ⓐ Jean has to give her dog a bath.

Ⓑ Jean, her mom, and Taz walk home.

Ⓒ A skunk sprays Jean, her mom, and Taz.

STOP

Read "A Solar Solution" before you answer Numbers 1 through 5.

A Solar Solution

"Do I have to go?" Kim asked. "Meetings are so boring."

Kim's mom was going to the town meeting.

"You can't stay home alone," Mom said. "Also, you might like it."

Many people were at the meeting. Kim saw some neighbors. She waved to Mrs. Mint, who lived next door.

Mayor Moss **insisted** that people be quiet. "Shhh," she said firmly.

The meeting began. First, the mayor talked about road signs. Kim was bored. She tried not to yawn.

Then Mayor Moss changed topics. "Our town hall uses a lot of electricity. How could we save money?"

GO ON →

Kim thought about her science class. She raised her hand.

The mayor nodded at her. "Please say your name. Then tell your idea."

Kim was nervous. "My name is Kim," she said. "We could get solar panels. I learned about them in school. They use sunlight to make electricity."

There was silence. Kim hoped people would not laugh.

"I think that's very **true**," the mayor said. "You're correct that solar panels will help save money."

The mayor asked people to vote. People who agreed raised their hands. The mayor counted. Kim's idea won!

Mom and Kim drove home.

"Kim, I think you liked the meeting," Mom said. "You showed that you have great ideas."

Kim smiled. She liked solving problems!

GO ON →

Use "A Solar Solution" to answer Numbers 1 through 5.

1 Which event happens FIRST?

Ⓐ Kim tells her idea.

Ⓑ The meeting begins.

Ⓒ Mom and Kim drive home.

2 Read these sentences from the story.

Mayor Moss *insisted* that people be quiet. "Shhh," she said firmly.

Which word helps you understand what *insisted* means?

Ⓐ that

Ⓑ firmly

Ⓒ people

3 What does Mayor Moss talk about FIRST?

Ⓐ road signs

Ⓑ town hall

Ⓒ Kim's idea

GO ON →

4 Read these sentences from the story.

"I think that's very *true*," the mayor said. "You're correct that solar panels will help save money."

Which word means about the SAME as *true*?

Ⓐ correct

Ⓑ panels

Ⓒ save

5 Which event happens LAST?

Ⓐ Mom and Kim drive home.

Ⓑ The mayor asks people to vote.

Ⓒ Kim hoped people would not laugh.

Read "Comets: A Special Sight" before you answer Numbers 6 through 10.

Comets: A Special Sight

Look at the sky at **nighttime**. It is dark. You may see stars. You may see the moon. On very special nights, you might see a comet!

Comets fly through space. They circle the Sun. There are many comets. But we see only a few. Sometimes comets come close to the Sun. Then we may see them.

A comet is a ball. It is made of ice and dust. It is like a dirty snowball. When a comet comes near the Sun, it changes. It gets a head and a tail. The tail is very long. A cloud forms around the head. This cloud is called a coma.

The word comet comes from a Greek word. It means "hairy head." A comet's head looks like a star. The tail looks like hair.

GO ON →

Comets are very old. People have seen them for a long time. A famous comet is Halley's Comet. We see it about every 75 years. People in China first saw it over 2,000 years ago.

You can see some comets easily. But others are harder to see. You might need a telescope.

Keep checking the sky. You may be lucky. You may see a comet!

Parts of a comet

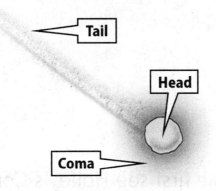

Tail

Head

Coma

GO ON →

Name: _____ Date: _____

Use "Comets: A Special Sight" to answer Numbers 6 through 10.

6 Read these sentences from the article.

> **Look at the sky in *nighttime*. It is dark. You may see stars.**

Which word helps you figure out what *nighttime* means?

Ⓐ dark

Ⓑ look

Ⓒ sky

7 What is a comet made of?

Ⓐ snow

Ⓑ ice and dust

Ⓒ stars and hair

8 When did people first see Halley's Comet?

Ⓐ 75 years ago

Ⓑ 500 years ago

Ⓒ 2,000 years ago

9 Why did the author MOST LIKELY write "Comets: A Special Sight"?

Ⓐ to tell readers about comets

Ⓑ to tell readers to look at the sky

Ⓒ to tell readers to buy a telescope

10 Look at the diagram on page 93. The diagram shows

Ⓐ that a comet is ice and dust.

Ⓑ that there are many comets.

Ⓒ the parts of a comet.

STOP

Read "The Desert" before you answer Numbers 1 through 6.

The Desert

Where is the hottest place on Earth? Is it in Africa? Is it in Asia? The hottest temperature was recorded in a desert. That desert is in California! It is the Mojave Desert.

Desert Climate

Deserts are very dry. They get less than 10 inches of rain a year. They are also very hot. But at night the desert can be cool.

The **seasons** are different in the desert. Summer is hot. Fall is warm. Winter may be cold and bring rain. Then flowers may grow in spring.

Desert Plants

Desert plants have to survive in the dry heat. They need to live with not much water. A cactus is one desert plant. It stores water. It does not have leaves. It has needles. Leaves lose water. Needles hold water.

GO ON →

Desert Animals

Animals learn to live in the heat. Lizards and snakes stay under rocks to keep cool. A pack rat builds a den with sticks. It stays in the shade. Many animals go out at night. That is when owls hunt.

Death Valley

Death Valley is in the Mojave Desert. A valley is the low space between mountains. Mountains trap the hot air. Death Valley is very low. It gets very hot. But the mountains may have snow on top.

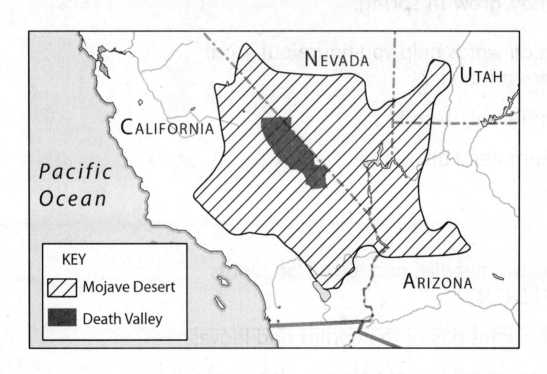

GO ON →

Name: _____ **Date:** _____

Use "The Desert" to answer Numbers 1 through 6.

1 How is night DIFFERENT from day?

Ⓐ It is drier at night.

Ⓑ It is cooler at night.

Ⓒ It is hotter at night.

2 Read these sentences from the article.

The *seasons* are different in the desert. Summer is hot. Fall is warm. Winter may be cold and bring rain. Then flowers may grow in spring.

Which words help you figure out what *seasons* means?

Ⓐ different, desert

Ⓑ Summer, Fall

Ⓒ then, may

3 How are needles and leaves on plants DIFFERENT?

Ⓐ A cactus has both needles and leaves.

Ⓑ Leaves hold water. Needles lose water.

Ⓒ Leaves lose water. Needles hold water.

Name: _____ Date: _____

4 Why do snakes stay under rocks?

Ⓐ They stay cool under rocks.

Ⓑ They stay warm under rocks.

Ⓒ They store water under rocks.

5 Why is Death Valley so hot?

Ⓐ A valley is a low space between mountains.

Ⓑ The mountains may have snow on top.

Ⓒ Mountains trap hot air in the valley.

6 What state is most of Death Valley located in?

Ⓐ California

Ⓑ Nevada

Ⓒ Arizona

Copyright © McGraw-Hill Education. Permission is granted to reproduce for classroom use.

Mid-Unit Assessment · Unit 4   Grade 2   **99**

Read "New School, New Sport" before you answer Numbers 7 through 10.

New School, New Sport

"Dad, I don't want to go," said Tim. Tim was nervous. It was his first day of school in the United States. His family had just moved here from England.

"It will be fine. You like school and sports. You will fit right in," said his father.

"I hope so. But I am sure things are different here," said Tim.

Tim walked to school. He thought about sports. He missed his **local** football team. The team that played near his home was the best! Football was called soccer here, Tim remembered. Soccer is England's most popular sport.

Tim got to school. He met a boy named Ron.

"What sport do you like to play?" asked Ron.

"I like to play football," said Tim.

"You play football in England? I did not know that," asked Ron.

"Oh, I'm sorry. We call football what you call soccer," said Tim.

GO ON →

"You like to play soccer. I get it," said Ron.

"Do you play soccer here?" asked Tim.

"Some kids play soccer. But I play baseball. Do you play baseball?" asked Ron.

"No, I don't know how to play baseball. It is not popular in England. I **wonder** what it is like to play. I think about it a lot," said Tim.

"Baseball is very popular here. And I will teach you how to play. I am the best player in this school," said Ron.

After school Ron and Tim went to the park. They played catch. The baseball glove was strange to Tim. But he liked baseball! He liked his new friend, Ron, too. Tim knew his new school would be fine.

GO ON →

Name: _____ **Date:** _____ →

Use "New School, New Sport" to answer
Numbers 7 through 10.

7 Read these sentences from the story.

> **He missed his *local* football team.
> The team that played near his home
> was the best!**

Which words help you figure out what
local means?

Ⓐ He missed

Ⓑ near his home

Ⓒ team that played

8 How are Tim and Ron ALIKE?

Ⓐ They are both from England.

Ⓑ They both like school.

Ⓒ They both like sports.

GO ON →

9 Read these sentences from the story.

> **"No, I don't know how to play baseball.
> It is not popular in England. I *wonder*
> what it is like to play. I think about it
> a lot," said Tim.**

Which words help you figure out what
wonder means?

Ⓐ not popular

Ⓑ think about it a lot

Ⓒ don't know how to play

10 How are Tim and Ron DIFFERENT?

Ⓐ Ron is from England. Tim is from the
United States.

Ⓑ Tim knows how to play baseball. Ron knows
how to play football.

Ⓒ Tim knows how to play soccer. Ron knows
how to play baseball.

STOP

Read "The Right Choice" before you answer Numbers I through 5.

The Right Choice

On Saturday, Rick and Rosa could not **agree**. They did not want to do the same thing. Rick wanted to play basketball in his driveway. Rosa wanted to help clean up the school playground. There was a lot of litter in the playground. A school group was holding a cleanup event.

Rick crossed his arms. "I don't want to go back to school on a Saturday!" he said. "Other people can help clean up the playground. Why do I have to?"

"But we love the playground!" Rosa said. "We should help clean it up. It's the right thing to do. Then we can play later."

"OK," Rick said. He sighed. It wasn't going to be such a fun day after all.

GO ON →

Rick's mom drove Rick and Rosa to the playground. Ms. Lott, a math teacher, was in charge. There were about 30 kids helping. They got special t-shirts. They got plastic bags and gloves. They used poles to grab trash. They worked hard for a few hours. Then the playground looked much cleaner.

The kids had a break. Ms. Lott brought out watermelon. Rick and Rosa laughed as they ate the sticky slices. They were **amused**. Then their friend Mark came over. He challenged Rick and Rosa to a game of tag. Now the lawn was clean. It was easy to run around.

Rosa's dad picked them up. Rick said, "Thanks, Rosa. I'm glad we helped. I feel good about the day."

Rosa smiled. "It's still light out. Do you feel like playing basketball? We could fit in a quick game," she said.

"Yes!" Rick said.

GO ON →

Name: _____ **Date:** _____

Use "The Right Choice" to answer Numbers 1 through 5.

1 Read these sentences from the story.

> **On Saturday, Rick and Rosa could not** *agree.* **They did not want to do the same thing.**

Which word helps you figure out what *agree* means?

Ⓐ could

Ⓑ same

Ⓒ Saturday

2 What is Rick's point of view at the BEGINNING?

Ⓐ He wants to clean up the playground.

Ⓑ He wants to play basketball.

Ⓒ He wants to play tag.

GO ON →

3 Why does Rosa want to clean up the playground?

　Ⓐ She doesn't like basketball.

　Ⓑ She wants to eat watermelon.

　Ⓒ They love the playground, so it is the right thing to do.

4 Read these sentences from the story.

Rick and Rosa laughed as they ate the sticky slices. They were *amused*.

Which word helps you figure out what *amused* means?

　Ⓐ laughed

　Ⓑ ate

　Ⓒ sticky

5 What is Rick's point of view at the END?

　Ⓐ He is glad he helped clean up the playground.

　Ⓑ He doesn't want to play basketball.

　Ⓒ He is mad at Rosa.

Read "Rosa Parks" before you answer Numbers 6 through 10.

Rosa Parks

Rosa Parks was born on February 4, 1913. She lived in Alabama. When she was born, things were not equal. Rosa was African-American. She could not go to the same schools as white children. She had to sit in the back of the bus. This was called segregation.

When Rosa was young, her mother taught her at home. Then she moved to Montgomery, Alabama. She lived with an aunt. She went to a private school. To pay for school, Rosa cleaned classrooms.

When Rosa grew up, she knew she had a **responsibility**. It was her duty to help change things. In 1943, she joined the NAACP. This was a group that fought for equal rights.

On December 1, 1955, Rosa rode on a bus. She sat in the back. A white man asked her to give up her seat. Rosa refused. This was against the city law. She was arrested. Rosa spent the night in jail. She was fined.

GO ON →

Rosa's arrest got a lot of attention. Martin Luther King, Jr. came to Montgomery. He started a boycott of the buses. Rosa helped, too. This meant that African-Americans would not ride buses. They walked or rode bikes instead. The boycott cost the buses a lot of money. It also helped change minds. In 1956, the Supreme Court ruled. It said that the bus law was wrong. After the ruling, Rosa rode on a bus. She sat right up front.

Rosa Parks was brave. She was a hero. Rosa showed that one person can have a big effect. Rosa helped change the way people thought.

Timeline of Rosa Parks' Life

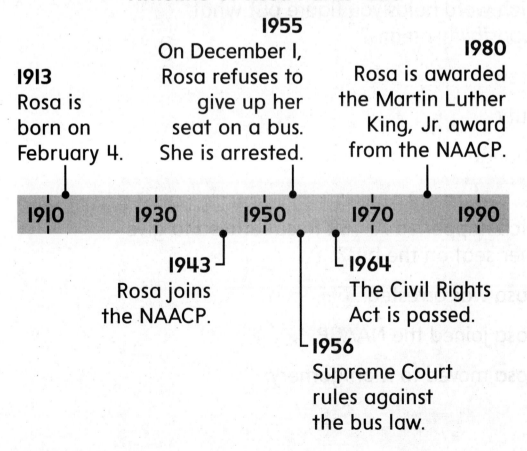

1913
Rosa is born on February 4.

1955
On December 1, Rosa refuses to give up her seat on a bus. She is arrested.

1980
Rosa is awarded the Martin Luther King, Jr. award from the NAACP.

1910   1930   1950   1970   1990

1943
Rosa joins the NAACP.

1964
The Civil Rights Act is passed.

1956
Supreme Court rules against the bus law.

GO ON →

Use "Rosa Parks" to answer Numbers 6 through 10.

6 Which event happened FIRST in Rosa's life?

Ⓐ Rosa cleaned classrooms to help pay for school.

Ⓑ Rosa helped plan a boycott.

Ⓒ Rosa joined the NAACP.

7 Read these sentences from the article.

When Rosa grew up, she knew she had a *responsibility*. It was her duty to help change things.

Which word helps you figure out what *responsibility* means?

Ⓐ grew

Ⓑ duty

Ⓒ change

8 Which happened AFTER Rosa refused to give up her seat on the bus?

Ⓐ Rosa was arrested.

Ⓑ Rosa joined the NAACP.

Ⓒ Rosa moved to Montgomery.

GO ON →

9 What happened AFTER the Montgomery bus boycott?

Ⓐ Rosa spent the night in jail.

Ⓑ Martin Luther King came to help.

Ⓒ The Supreme Court said the city bus law was wrong.

10 Look at the timeline. When did Rosa Parks win an award from the NAACP?

Ⓐ 1956

Ⓑ 1964

Ⓒ 1980

STOP

Read "Water Wheels" before you answer Numbers 1 through 5.

Water Wheels

People like rivers. Rivers are beautiful. They are also powerful. Ancient people saw rivers and wondered. How could they capture a river's **energy**? How could they use it to do work? Then, they found an answer. It was the water wheel.

Running water turns a water wheel. The wheel does work. Some wheels move water from one place to another. These are water-lifting wheels. Other water wheels are mill wheels. Mill wheels are part of machines. These machines grind things. They may grind grain into flour. People use flour to make bread.

Water-lifting Wheels

A water-lifting wheel was built in a river. The river pushed the wheel. This made the wheel turn. The wheel held buckets. The buckets filled with water. They poured the water into a canal, or ditch. Water flowed in the canal. The canal carried water to a farm. A farmer used it to water crops.

GO ON →

Mill Wheels

Mill wheels are water wheels that are part of a machine. A river turns the water wheel. The water wheel turns a gear. The gear turns another wheel. This wheel can do work. A grist mill grinds wheat. The wheat becomes flour. A paper mill grinds up wood. This makes paper. A saw mill wheel moves a saw that cuts wood.

Water wheels might seem simple. But they are important. They changed how we use nature. They changed the way we live and work.

How a grist mill works

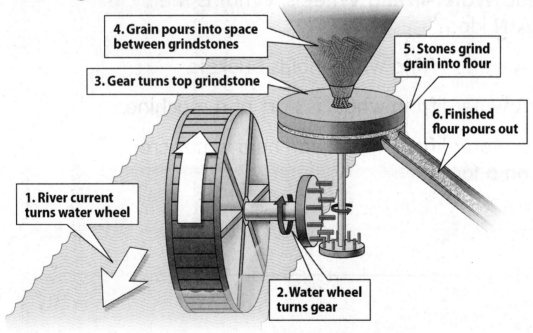

4. Grain pours into space between grindstones

3. Gear turns top grindstone

5. Stones grind grain into flour

6. Finished flour pours out

1. River current turns water wheel

2. Water wheel turns gear

GO ON →

Name: _____ **Date:** _____ →

Use "Water Wheels" to answer Numbers 1 through 5.

1 Read these sentences from the article.

> **How could they capture a river's *energy*? How could they use it to do work? Then, they found an answer.**

Which words help you figure out what *energy* means?

Ⓐ could they capture

Ⓑ use it to do work

Ⓒ found an answer

2 Read **Water-lifting Wheels**. What is the MAIN idea?

Ⓐ A water-lifting wheel holds buckets.

Ⓑ A water-lifting wheel is part of a machine.

Ⓒ A water-lifting wheel can help water crops on a farm.

GO ON →

3 What is the MAIN idea of Mill Wheels?

Ⓐ A river turns the water wheel.

Ⓑ The water wheel turns a gear.

Ⓒ Mill wheels are water wheels that are part of a machine.

4 Look at the diagram. What happens AFTER the grain pours into the space between the grindstones?

Ⓐ The water wheel turns the gear.

Ⓑ The stones grind the grain into flour.

Ⓒ The river current turns the water wheel.

5 What is the author's purpose for writing this article?

Ⓐ to tell how to build water wheels

Ⓑ to tell why people should use water wheels more often

Ⓒ to tell how water wheels changed the way we live and work

GO ON →

Read "Demeter and Kore" before you answer Numbers 6 through 10.

Demeter and Kore

Long ago, Demeter ruled over the Earth's plants. Her job was very **important**. People needed crops to live. Demeter had a daughter named Kore. Demeter loved Kore very much.

One day, King Hades was walking in a field. He saw Kore. She was now a beautiful young woman. Her **golden** hair shone like the sun. Hades fell deeply in love. He took Kore to his kingdom under the Earth.

Demeter was worried. Kore had not come home. Demeter searched high and low. But she could not find Kore. Demeter became sad. And while Demeter was sad, no crops grew.

Deep in the underworld, Kore was unhappy. Hades tried to cheer her up. He gave her a pomegranate to eat. Kore knew it was a trick. People in the underworld could not eat. If they ate, they had to stay forever. But months passed. Kore's hunger grew. One day, she ate six pomegranate seeds. She had to stay forever.

GO ON →

Meanwhile, Zeus was not pleased. Zeus ruled over the Earth and Sky. No crops were growing. His kingdom was in ruins. Something had to be done. So he went to Hades. He demanded that Hades return Kore to Demeter. Hades made a deal with Zeus. Each year, Kore would spend six months on Earth. The other six months, she would live in the underworld. Zeus agreed.

Now, Kore stays underground half the year. Demeter and the people on Earth wait patiently. Then, Kore returns. Demeter becomes happy again. Life blooms everywhere. Kore's golden hair shines in the fields. People harvest the fruits, grains, and vegetables they need to live.

GO ON →

Use "Demeter and Kore" to answer Numbers 6 through 10.

6 Read these sentences from the story.

> **Long ago, Demeter ruled over the Earth's plants. Her job was very *important*. People needed crops to live. Demeter had a daughter named Kore.**

Which words help you figure out what *important* means?

Ⓐ the Earth's plants

Ⓑ needed crops to live

Ⓒ had a daughter

7 Read these sentences from the story.

> **She was now a beautiful young woman. Her *golden* hair shone like the sun. Hades fell deeply in love.**

Which words help you figure out what *golden* means?

Ⓐ shone like the sun

Ⓑ fell deeply in love

Ⓒ beautiful young woman

GO ON →

8 Why do no crops grow?

Ⓐ Demeter is sad.

Ⓑ Kore is unhappy.

Ⓒ Zeus is not pleased.

9 What deal does Hades make with Zeus?

Ⓐ Kore will spend one year in the underworld. Then she will spend the next year on Earth.

Ⓑ Each year, Kore will spend six months with Hades in the underworld. Then she will spend six months with Demeter on Earth.

Ⓒ Hades will give Kore back if Demeter will make the crops grow again.

10 What is the message in this story?

Ⓐ to explain why Kore's hair is golden

Ⓑ to explain why plants grow only half the year

Ⓒ to explain how to harvest fruits, grains, and vegetables

STOP

8. Why do no crops grow?

Ⓐ Demeter is sad

Ⓑ Kore is unhappy

Ⓒ Zeus is not pleased

9. What deal does Hades make with Zeus?

Ⓐ Kore will spend one year in the underworld. Then she will spend the next year on Earth.

Ⓑ Each year, Kore will spend six months with Hades in the underworld. Then she will spend six months with Demeter on earth.

Ⓒ Hades will give Kore back if Demeter will make the crops grow again.

10. What is the message in this story?

Ⓐ to explain why Kore's hair is golden

Ⓑ to explain why plants grow only half the year

Ⓒ to explain how to harvest fruits, grains, and vegetables

Unit
Assessment

Read "Tom Rakes Leaves" before you answer Numbers I through 8.

Tom Rakes Leaves

Mom asks Tom for help.

She asks Tom to rake leaves.

But Tom does not like to rake.

The leaves fall from a big tree.

The tree is next door.

It is filled with leaves.

It is filled with plums.

Mom tells Tom to **choose**.

He may rake leaves.

He may wash dishes.

Tom must pick.

Tom takes a **glance** at the sink.

He sees six plates.

He sees ten mugs.

He sees five pans.

He sees lots of pots.

Tom makes up his mind.

GO ON →

Tom gets the rake.

He rakes and rakes.

He makes a big pile.

Then a big wind blows.

Leaves fly!

The leaves will not stay in place!

Tom sees his pal Nat.

Nat has a rake.

He has a big bag.

Nat will help.

Tom is glad.

Nat rakes. Tom bags.

Soon not a leaf is left.

Tom smiles.

He sees Mrs. Lane.

Mrs. Lane is Nat's mom.

She has a plum cake.

She will **share** it.

Mrs. Lane gives Tom a slice.

Mrs. Lane gives Nat a slice.

It has been a fun day!

GO ON →

Use "Tom Rakes Leaves" to answer Numbers 1 through 8.

1 Who is the MAIN character in the story?

Ⓐ Tom

Ⓑ Nat

Ⓒ Mom

2 Who asks for help?

Ⓐ Nat

Ⓑ Nat's mom

Ⓒ Tom's mom

3 What helps Tom make up his mind?

Ⓐ He likes to rake leaves.

Ⓑ There are a lot of dirty dishes.

Ⓒ Mrs. Lane gives him a slice of cake.

GO ON →

4 Which word means the SAME as *choose*?

Ⓐ tells

Ⓑ sink

Ⓒ pick

5 Which word helps explain what *glance* means?

Ⓐ sees

Ⓑ makes

Ⓒ gets

6 What does Nat do?

Ⓐ Nat washes dishes.

Ⓑ Nat rakes leaves.

Ⓒ Nat bags leaves.

GO ON →

7 Which detail tells that the raking is finished?

Ⓐ stay in place

Ⓑ has a big bag

Ⓒ not a leaf is left

8 How does Mrs. Lane *share* the plum cake?

Ⓐ She sees Tom.

Ⓑ She has a plum cake.

Ⓒ She gives slices to Tom and Nat.

GO ON →

Read "Pet Shop" before you answer Numbers 9 through 15.

Pet Shop

Beth goes to the pet shop.
Which pet will she get?

A pup is a cute pet.
The pup runs.
It is very playful.
The pup has a leash.

A crab has a hard shell.
Can a crab be a pet?
Beth watches its **actions.**
The crab digs in the sand.
It hunts for food.

Beth sees a big snake.
This pet is long.
The snake slides.
It sleeps in a big cage.

A soft cat can be a good pet.
It plays with a fun toy.
Beth pats the cat.
The cat purrs.

GO ON →

Can a bird be a nice pet?

The bird can talk.

The bird can say hi.

It can say bye.

It has a cage with a swing.

Beth sees some fish.

They are in a tank.

The red fish has big fins.

The fish swims and dives.

It eats food flakes.

Then Beth sees a furry rabbit.

It hops and hides.

Beth asks a question.

"What are this pet's **needs**?"

It needs food and water.

It also needs hugs!

This is the pet for Beth!

GO ON →

Use "Pet Shop" to answer Numbers 9 through 15.

9 Which pet has a leash?

Ⓐ a pup

Ⓑ a crab

Ⓒ a bird

10 What are a crab's *actions*?

Ⓐ It has a shell.

Ⓑ It digs and hunts.

Ⓒ It slides and sleeps.

11 Which word tells about a snake?

Ⓐ long

Ⓑ purrs

Ⓒ soft

12 What does Beth do?

Ⓐ She sleeps in a cage.

Ⓑ She plays with a toy.

Ⓒ She pats the cat.

GO ON →

13 Why does a bird make a nice pet?

Ⓐ It can talk.

Ⓑ It has a cage.

Ⓒ It has a swing.

14 Which pet has big fins?

Ⓐ the snake

Ⓑ the red fish

Ⓒ the furry rabbit

15 What *needs* does a rabbit have?

Ⓐ a place to swim

Ⓑ to ask a question

Ⓒ food, water, and hugs

STOP

Read "Bird and Lion" before you answer Numbers I through 8.

Bird and Lion

It is a quiet day. The sky is bright blue. A few birds fly up and down. They try to catch fish in the river.

Lion moves through the tall grass. She is angry. She wants to hunt, but her father says she must wait. She is too young. The other lions do not need her help.

Lion looks up at the sky. A bird makes a loud noise. He falls to the grass. Everything is still and quiet. The **silence** makes Lion nervous.

Bird opens one eye. He cannot get up. He has trouble breathing. He looks at Lion. He needs to **escape** and get away from her!

Lion is still angry, but she does not hunt Bird. She feels sorry for Bird. Lion sits down. She guards Bird.

GO ON →

Bird gets up slowly. Bird thanks Lion for not hunting him. He says one day he will help her.

Lion laughs at Bird. Bird is too small to help her. What can a little bird do?

A year passes. Lion returns from a hunt. She moves to the river for a drink. The water is cool.

She hears a sound. It comes from the sky. Bird flies near Lion's head. Bird squawks at Lion. He tells her to run. Lion jumps back.

Crocodile slams down near her. He snaps at Lion with pointed teeth. Lion runs far from him. Bird has saved her!

Lion has learned a lesson. Bird may be small, but he helped her. Lion thanks Bird.

GO ON →

Use "Bird and Lion" to answer Numbers I through 8.

1 What problem does Lion have at the BEGINNING of the story?

Ⓐ Lion wants to catch fish in the river.

Ⓑ Lion's father will not let her hunt.

Ⓒ The other lions need her help.

2 Read these sentences from the story.

A bird makes a loud noise. He falls to the grass. Everything is still and quiet. The *silence* makes Lion nervous.

Which words help explain what *silence* means?

Ⓐ still and quiet

Ⓑ falls to the grass

Ⓒ makes a loud noise

3 What happens to Bird?

Ⓐ Bird looks up at the bright blue sky.

Ⓑ Bird makes a soft noise in the tall grass.

Ⓒ Bird falls to the grass and cannot get up.

GO ON →

4 Read these sentences from the story.

> **He has trouble breathing. He looks at Lion. He needs to *escape* and get away from her!**

Which words are a clue to what *escape* means?

Ⓐ trouble breathing

Ⓑ get away from

Ⓒ looks at

5 Why does Bird say he will help Lion?

Ⓐ to thank Lion for not hunting him

Ⓑ to get away from Lion

Ⓒ to make Lion angry

6 How does Bird help Lion?

Ⓐ Bird squawks at Crocodile.

Ⓑ Bird jumps up and down.

Ⓒ Bird tells Lion to run.

GO ON →

7 Why does Lion change her mind about Bird?

   Ⓐ Bird flies near Lion.

   Ⓑ Bird has saved Lion.

   Ⓒ Bird cannot help Lion.

8 What happens LAST in the story?

   Ⓐ Lion thanks Bird.

   Ⓑ Bird learns a lesson.

   Ⓒ Crocodile snaps at Lion.

Read "Polar Bears: Life on the Ice" before you answer Numbers 9 through 15.

Polar Bears: Life on the Ice

Polar bears live in the Arctic. It is a cold place. Ice floats in the water. There are no trees. How do polar bears stay warm? They have adapted to the cold.

What They Look Like

Polar bears are **giant,** or very large. Males grow up to 1,700 pounds. They can be 10 feet tall. They may live 25 years.

Their **fur** has no color. It looks white in the snow. Fur is thick hair. It grows on skin.

They have black skin. Their skin soaks up the Sun's rays. This helps warm them.

Fat traps heat. Polar bears have a lot of fat. It helps them stay warm, too.

GO ON →

Why They Hunt

Cubs are born in dens. Dens are warm. Their mother cares for them. She protects them for 28 months. They learn to hunt.

They hunt seals. Seals go under the sea ice. They come up for air. Polar bears wait on the sea ice. Then they grab the seals.

Polar bears eat what they want. No one can compete with them.

It is still hard to find food, though. Arctic water is warming up. Sea ice melts too soon. Polar bears do not have time to hunt. They swim to find more sea ice. They go far from home.

How You Can Help

What can you do? Learn about polar bears. Talk to friends about them. Write to people who protect animals. **Express** your thoughts. Tell them how you feel. Ask them to speak for you.

GO ON →

Use "Polar Bears: Life on the Ice" to answer Numbers 9 through 15.

9 What is the MAIN topic of this article?

Ⓐ how much polar bears weigh

Ⓑ how to write about polar bears

Ⓒ how polar bears live in the Arctic

10 Read these sentences from the article.

Polar bears are *giant*, or very large. Males grow up to 1,700 pounds.

Which word is a clue to what *giant* means?

Ⓐ bears

Ⓑ large

Ⓒ pounds

11 Which words mean about the SAME as *fur*?

Ⓐ on skin

Ⓑ no color

Ⓒ thick hair

GO ON →

12 Which key detail tells one way polar bears keep warm?

Ⓐ There are no trees.

Ⓑ It grows on skin.

Ⓒ Fat traps heat.

13 Which heading would you use to find out about something polar bears do?

Ⓐ Why They Hunt

Ⓑ How You Can Help

Ⓒ What They Look Like

14 Why it is hard for polar bears to find food?

Ⓐ Seals come up for air.

Ⓑ They have to swim to find ice.

Ⓒ These bears eat what they want.

15 Which word from the article means almost the SAME as *express*?

Ⓐ about

Ⓑ learn

Ⓒ speak

STOP

Read "In the Air" before you answer Numbers I through 7.

In the Air

"Why was the sunset such a strange color?" Jan asked her teacher. "It was pink."

"Good question," Ms. Son answered. "It is because of pollution."

"What is that?" asked Rob.

"Pollution is bad gas in the air. Do you know the smelly fumes a car makes? That is pollution," she explained.

"Really?" asked Alex. "Where else does pollution come from?"

"Buses make it. Factories make it. Fires make it," she said.

"Then what happens?" Rob asked.

Ms. Son said, "There is a layer of good air in the sky. It is the ozone layer."

The class wanted to know more.

GO ON →

"It protects us from the sun. Pollution harms this layer," Ms. Son replied.

"I want to **prevent** pollution," Alex said. "I want to stop it."

"What can you do?" Ms. Son asked the class.

"I will make a sign. I will put it in a parking lot. It will ask drivers to take a bus. Less traffic means cleaner air," Jan said.

"Good," replied Ms. Son. "Does anyone else have an idea?"

"My next door **neighbor** drives a school bus. It stays on a lot. I will ask her to turn it off. That will make less pollution," said Alex.

Rob said, "I will write a story. I will put it in the school paper. It will tell kids about pollution."

"That is a good start. We can work together. We can help make the air clean," said Ms. Son.

GO ON →

Use "In the Air" to answer Numbers I through 7.

1 What happens FIRST in the story?

Ⓐ Alex asks where pollution comes from.

Ⓑ Jan asks about the pink sunset.

Ⓒ Rob asks what pollution is.

2 What does Ms. Son do right BEFORE she talks about smelly fumes from cars?

Ⓐ She tells what pollution is.

Ⓑ She asks the class for ideas.

Ⓒ She says cars make pollution.

3 When does the class want to know more?

Ⓐ after Ms. Son tells what the ozone layer is

Ⓑ when Ms. Son says they can work together

Ⓒ before Ms. Son talks about the ozone layer

4 Which word from the story means about the SAME as *prevent*?

Ⓐ pollution

Ⓑ want

Ⓒ stop

GO ON →

5 Who has the FIRST idea?

Ⓐ Jan

Ⓑ Alex

Ⓒ Rob

6 Read this sentence from the story.

My next door *neighbor* drives a school bus. It stays on a lot.

Which words help you know what *neighbor* means?

Ⓐ next door

Ⓑ school bus

Ⓒ stays on a lot

7 Who gives the LAST idea?

Ⓐ Alex

Ⓑ Rob

Ⓒ Jan

GO ON →

Read "Monsoon!" before you answer Numbers 8 through 15.

Monsoon!

Feel that strong breeze? Hear the rain hit the roof? It is that time of year. Here comes the monsoon!

Big Rains in Asia

In parts of Asia there are big storms. They are called monsoons. They can happen in summer or winter. These storms can have a lot of rain.

In summer, cool winds blow over land. The air has lots of water. This water falls as rain. In winter, winds blow away from land. These storms have less rain.

The Good and the Bad

Monsoons can be good. Farmers like the rain. Rain helps crops grow. There is more food to eat. There is more food to sell. Too little rain can be bad. Crops will not grow. There is less to eat. There is less to sell. Life is better with more rain.

GO ON →

But monsoons also can be bad. Too much rain can cause floods. Flood waters do not move at a slow **speed**. They move at a fast rate of motion. They are strong, too. Floods can **destroy**, or ruin, property. They can wipe out small towns and **villages**. Farms are lost. Roads wash away. There is less food.

Western Monsoons

Asia is not the only place with these big storms. There are monsoons in the West, too. They are in Arizona.

They take place in summer. Cool, wet winds cause storms. There is a lot of rain and dust. There are bad floods.

Arizona is very dry. Farmers need this rain. Much of their water comes from these storms. They help crops grow. They also help fight forest fires.

GO ON ➔

Name: _____ **Date:** _____

Use "Monsoon!" to answer Numbers 8 through 15.

8 Which sentence from the article tells when monsoons happen in Asia?

Ⓐ It is that time of year.

Ⓑ In parts of Asia there are big storms.

Ⓒ They can happen in summer or winter.

9 What does the author want you to know about monsoons?

Ⓐ They hit the roof.

Ⓑ They are good and bad.

Ⓒ They are caused by floods.

10 Which part of the article tells about the effects of monsoons?

Ⓐ **Monsoon!**

Ⓑ **Big Rains in Asia**

Ⓒ **The Good and the Bad**

11 Read these sentences from the article.

> **Flood waters do not move at a slow _speed_. They move at a fast rate of motion.**

Which words help you understand what _speed_ means?

Ⓐ flood waters

Ⓑ do not move

Ⓒ rate of motion

12 Read these sentences from the article.

> **They are strong, too. Floods can _destroy_, or ruin, property.**

Which word means the SAME as _destroy_?

Ⓐ ruin

Ⓑ floods

Ⓒ strong

GO ON →

13 Read these sentences from the article.

> **They can wipe out small towns and *villages*. Farms are lost. Roads wash away.**

Which words mean about the SAME as *villages*?

Ⓐ wipe out

Ⓑ small towns

Ⓒ wash away

14 What is the MAIN idea of the **Western Monsoons** section of the article?

Ⓐ There are monsoons in Arizona.

Ⓑ Asia is the only place for monsoons.

Ⓒ Monsoons can help fight forest fires.

15 Why did the author MOST LIKELY write this article?

Ⓐ to tell why farmers in Asia like monsoons

Ⓑ to describe how monsoons helps crops

Ⓒ to give information about monsoons

STOP

Read "Moths and Butterflies" before you answer Numbers I through 7.

Moths and Butterflies

Callie was happy. Today her class had a field trip. They would visit a butterfly and moth sanctuary, or shelter. Callie loved to see nature up close.

Many kinds of butterflies and moths lived there. They were taken care of. The shelter was not **outdoors.** It was covered in glass. Mr. Green led the class through it.

They passed colorful flowers. Many tiny winged creatures flew in the air. Mr. Green stopped by a butterfly. It was sitting on a leaf.

"This is a monarch butterfly," he said. "Look at how colorful it is. It is orange, black, and white. These colors tell other animals not to eat it!"

Just then, Callie saw another animal land on a leaf. "Look!" she said.

Mr. Green said, "Thanks, Callie. This animal is an Imperial moth. Moths and butterflies have many **similarities.** But they are also different. What looks the same about these two animals?"

GO ON →

Callie raised her hand. "They both have wings. They have six legs."

"That's very good!" Mr. Green said. "See the two feelers coming out of their heads? Butterflies have little clubs or balls on the ends. The feelers on moths look like little feathers. Another difference is their color. Which is more colorful?"

Another student, Max, raised his hand. He said, "The butterfly is more colorful. The moth is gray."

"Good job, Max," Mr. Green said. "Moths are more active at night. They want to blend in."

On the bus ride home, Callie sat next to Max. She asked what his favorite was. He liked the moth.

He asked, "Which one did you like most?"

Callie liked the butterfly. "But the very best part," she said, "was learning from looking at nature!"

GO ON →

Use "Moths and Butterflies" to answer Numbers I through 7.

1 Which sentence from the story tells why Callie is happy about her class field trip?

Ⓐ Callie loved to see nature up close.

Ⓑ Mr. Green led the class through it.

Ⓒ They passed colorful flowers.

2 Read these sentences from the story.

They were taken care of. The shelter was not *outdoors*. It was covered in glass.

Which words are a clue to what *outdoors* means?

Ⓐ taken care of

Ⓑ shelter was not

Ⓒ covered in glass

3 Read these sentences from the story.

Moths and butterflies have many *similarities*. But they are also different.

Which word means about the OPPOSITE of *similarities*?

Ⓐ also

Ⓑ many

Ⓒ different

GO ON →

4 What is the SAME when the story begins and
     when it ends?

Ⓐ Max does not like moths.

Ⓑ Callie likes to look at nature.

Ⓒ Mr. Green talks about antennae.

5 How are butterflies and moths DIFFERENT?

Ⓐ Butterflies and moths both fly in the air.

Ⓑ Butterflies are more colorful than moths.

Ⓒ They have feelers that look like feathers.

6 How are Callie and Max ALIKE on the trip?

Ⓐ They both answer questions.

Ⓑ They both want to blend in.

Ⓒ They both are very quiet.

7 What is the lesson of this story?

Ⓐ Butterflies are better than moths.

Ⓑ Teachers take their classes on field trips.

Ⓒ You can learn a lot from looking at nature.

GO ON →

Read "Iceland" before you answer Numbers 8 through 15.

Iceland

Have you ever been to Iceland? Iceland is an island. It is **surrounded** by water. Iceland is in the middle of the ocean. It is not covered in ice!

Iceland has different areas. Each **region** has different features. The north is colder than the south. Both are good for farming. Most farmers in Iceland raise animals. A few raise crops.

The east and west are good for fishing. They both have *fjords*. That is where **steep** cliffs drop to the sea. The sharp slope of the cliffs means the water is very deep. It is perfect for boats. So, people fish there.

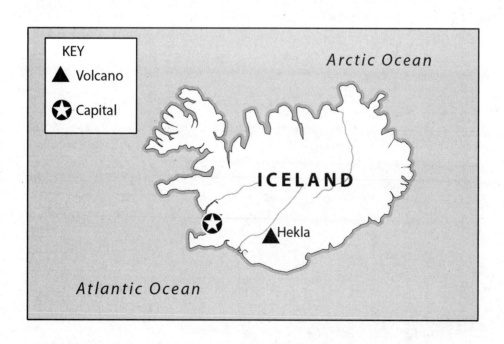

KEY
▲ Volcano
★ Capital

Arctic Ocean

ICELAND

★

▲ Hekla

Atlantic Ocean

GO ON →

All of the regions share one thing. Volcanoes are everywhere! Volcanoes are what formed Iceland. Iceland has around 200 volcanoes. They erupt often. One volcano is called Hekla. Hekla has erupted four times since 1947.

Iceland has many hot springs. These are pools of water. The volcanoes make the water warm. People swim in the hot springs. Hot springs bring a lot of visitors to Iceland.

Iceland does not have many animals. At first, foxes were the only mammals there. Other mammals are there now. People brought them. They are mostly farm animals. There are also mice and rats.

Iceland is an unusual place. But it is beautiful. There are lots of things that make it great to see.

GO ON →

Use "Iceland" to answer Numbers 8 through 15.

8 Which sentence from the article is a clue to what *surrounded* means?

Ⓐ Iceland is in the middle of the ocean.

Ⓑ Have you ever been to Iceland?

Ⓒ It is not covered in ice!

9 Read these sentences from the article.

Iceland has different areas. Each *region* has different features.

Which word has about the SAME meaning as *region*?

Ⓐ areas

Ⓑ different

Ⓒ features

10 How is the north of Iceland DIFFERENT from the south?

Ⓐ The north is colder than the south.

Ⓑ The north has more *fjords* than the south.

Ⓒ The north has more farming than the south.

GO ON →

11 Why are the east and west good for fishing?

   Ⓐ Volcanoes are all around.

   Ⓑ There are few crops.

   Ⓒ The water is deep.

12 Read these sentences from the article.

> **That is where *steep* cliffs drop to the sea. The sharp slope of the cliffs means the water is very deep.**

Which words help you understand what *steep* means?

   Ⓐ to the sea

   Ⓑ sharp slope

   Ⓒ is very deep

13 What feature is found in all areas of Iceland?

   Ⓐ fjords

   Ⓑ fishing

   Ⓒ volcanoes

GO ON →

14 What effect did people have on animals in Iceland?

Ⓐ They brought farm animals.

Ⓑ Foxes were the only mammals.

Ⓒ Mice and rats were the first animals.

15 Look at the map and map key. What does the dark triangle next to Hekla tell you?

Ⓐ Hekla is the capital.

Ⓑ Hekla is in Iceland.

Ⓒ Hekla is a volcano.

Read "A New Band in Town" before you answer Numbers 1 through 8.

A New Band in Town

Emily Marshall is writing a new song for the piano. She wants to be like her mother. Emily's mother is a musician. She plays the piano at concerts around the world.

Emily can't wait to perform for people. She knows she needs more practice. She talks to her band teacher after class.

"Mr. Young, I need your help! I like writing songs. How can I get people to listen to them?"

"Can you **describe** the songs you write? Tell me about them in words," Mr. Young says.

"I write about things that I know," she says. "I write about school. I write about how hard it is to move to a new place."

Mr. Young thinks for a moment. "Why not start a band? I have two new students. They might play with you. Have you met Keith or Dev?"

Emily meets Keith and Dev. Keith plays the drums. Dev plays the guitar. He also sings. They talk about music for hours. They agree to start a band.

GO ON →

They meet at Dev's house on the weekend. They **discover**, or find out, that picking a name is hard.

"We should name the band after me," Emily says. "I write the music. I like the name Marshall and Friends."

Dev frowns. "I don't think so. We should name the band after the singer."

"We need a name that we all like," Keith says. "We are new to Fallbrook. That is one thing we have in common."

Emily agrees. Fallbrook is a good name for the band.

Fallbrook practices for three months. Keith and Dev give Emily ideas for new songs.

Fallbrook plays for Mr. Young after school. He smiles and claps loudly. He asks them to play a concert for one of his classes.

Emily can't wait to tell her mother!

GO ON →

Use "A New Band in Town" to answer Numbers I through 8.

1 What is Emily's problem?

   Ⓐ Emily's mother is a musician.

   Ⓑ Emily does not want to play the piano.

   Ⓒ Emily wants people to listen to her songs.

2 Which sentence from the story explains what *describe* means?

   Ⓐ She talks to her band teacher after class.

   Ⓑ "Tell me about them in words."

   Ⓒ Mr. Young thinks for a moment.

3 What helps Emily solve her problem?

   Ⓐ Mr. Young thinks she should form a band.

   Ⓑ Emily writes about things she knows.

   Ⓒ Her mother plays the piano.

4 What does *discover* mean in the story?

   Ⓐ find out

   Ⓑ talk about

   Ⓒ pick a name

GO ON →

5 What is Emily's point of view about naming the new band?

Ⓐ She thinks it will be easy.

Ⓑ She asks Mr. Young to pick a name.

Ⓒ She wants to name the band after herself.

6 Why does Dev frown?

Ⓐ He does not like the name Emily suggests.

Ⓑ He wants to write songs for the band.

Ⓒ He wants Keith to name the band.

7 How does Keith solve the band's problem?

Ⓐ He agrees to start a band.

Ⓑ He thinks of a name they all like.

Ⓒ He and Dev give Emily ideas for songs.

8 Which sentence from the story is a clue to Mr. Young's point of view about the band?

Ⓐ They talk about music for hours.

Ⓑ Fallbrook plays for Mr. Young after school.

Ⓒ He asks them to play a concert for one of his classes.

GO ON →

Read "Teacher and Friend" before you answer
Numbers 9 through 15.

Teacher and Friend

Anne Sullivan was a teacher. She taught a girl named Helen Keller. It was a very big job. It was an **enormous** task.

Anne was born in 1866. Her mother died when she was eight. As a result, her father sent her to a special home. Anne was blind in one eye. So the home sent her to a school for people who could not see.

Her teachers knew Anne was smart. They asked her to help teach the younger kids. Anne finished school. Then she got a job with the Kellers. They lived far away. The **distance** was more than 1,000 miles. The Kellers wanted Anne to help their daughter, Helen. Helen was six.

Helen was sick when she was a baby. After that, she could not see or hear. She did not know the names for things she used. She did not know what a doll was. She did not know what water was. Anne wanted Helen to form pictures of things in her mind. She wanted Helen to use her **imagination.**

GO ON →

Anne put her fingers in Helen's hands. She drew letters with them. Helen learned the letters for "water." Then Anne put Helen's hand in water. Helen spelled the word in Anne's hand. She knew what it was! Anne taught Helen many more words.

Soon, Anne took Helen to school. It was the same school Anne had gone to. People wanted to know how Anne taught Helen. Helen and Anne became famous.

Anne was Helen's friend and teacher for almost 50 years. She helped Helen have a good life. People still talk about Anne today.

Anne and Helen

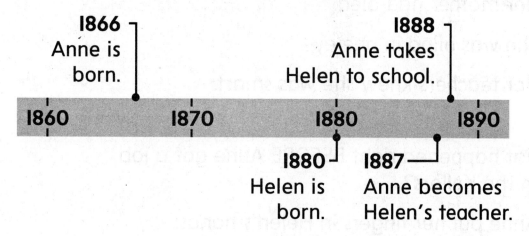

1866
Anne is born.

1888
Anne takes Helen to school.

1860   1870   1880   1890

1880
Helen is born.

1887
Anne becomes Helen's teacher.

GO ON →

Use "Teacher and Friend" to answer Numbers 9 through 15.

9 Read these sentences from the article.

> **It was a very big job. It was an *enormous* task.**

Which word means about the SAME as *enormous*?

Ⓐ big

Ⓑ job

Ⓒ task

10 Why did Anne's father send her to a special home?

Ⓐ Her mother had died.

Ⓑ She was blind in one eye.

Ⓒ Her teachers knew she was smart.

11 What happened right BEFORE Anne got a job with the Kellers?

Ⓐ Anne put her fingers in Helen's hands.

Ⓑ Soon, Anne took Helen to school.

Ⓒ Anne finished school.

12 Read these sentences from the article.

> **They lived far away. The *distance* was more than 1,000 miles. The Kellers wanted Anne to help their daughter, Helen.**

Which words give you a clue about what *distance* means?

Ⓐ far away

Ⓑ was more

Ⓒ their daughter

13 Read these sentences from the article.

> **She did not know what water was. Anne wanted Helen to form pictures of things in her mind. She wanted Helen to use her *imagination*.**

Which words help you understand what *imagination* means?

Ⓐ did not know what water was

Ⓑ pictures of things in her mind

Ⓒ wanted Helen to use

GO ON →

14 What happened as a result of Anne putting Helen's hand in water and spelling the word?

Ⓐ Helen got a new doll.

Ⓑ Helen helped younger kids.

Ⓒ Helen knew what water was.

15 Look at the timeline. When was Helen born?

Ⓐ 1866

Ⓑ 1880

Ⓒ 1888

STOP

Read "Why Roses Have Thorns" before you answer Numbers 1 through 6.

Why Roses Have Thorns

Long ago, wild roses did not have thorns. They grew on bushes with smooth stems. Their leaves **rustled** in the wind. The fragrant pink flowers covered the bushes. They were beautiful. They were also tasty. The Rabbits ate grass. But they also liked to nibble flowers. They liked to chew leaves. They ate entire bushes. Soon only a few Rose Bushes were left in the whole world.

The Rose Bushes had a meeting. They decided to go see Trickster. They would ask him for help. Trickster was a strange creature. He got angry quickly. And he was hard to find. The Rose Bushes agreed to look for him. They flew away on the wind. Soon they met a bird. "Trickster is in that valley," the bird said. "He is planting a garden."

The Rose Bushes were happy. They told the wind to blow them to the valley. As they neared, they heard Trickster shouting. He was very angry. The Rose Bushes were scared. They hid behind some trees.

GO ON →

A week before, Trickster had planted roses in his garden. They were covered with pink flowers. Then he had gone away. Just before the Rose Bushes arrived, he had returned. He found that the Rabbits had eaten his roses.

Now the Rose Bushes knew why Trickster was angry. They left their hiding place. Trickster was surprised to see them. He thought that all Rose Bushes had been eaten. Trickster listened. He thought for a minute about what to do. He decided in just a few **seconds**. He gave the Rose Bushes thorns to cover their stems. Now the Rabbits would not be able to eat them. Trickster sent the Rose Bushes home on the wind.

Ever since that day, all wild roses have had many thorns.

GO ON →

Name: _____ Date: _____

Use "Why Roses Have Thorns" to answer Numbers 1 through 6.

1 Read these sentences from the story.

They grew on bushes with smooth stems. Their leaves *rustled* in the wind.

Which word helps explain what *rustled* means?

Ⓐ bushes

Ⓑ stems

Ⓒ wind

2 Which sentence is a clue to the lesson the story teaches?

Ⓐ The Rose Bushes had a meeting.

Ⓑ They decided to go see Trickster.

Ⓒ Trickster was a strange creature.

3 Why do the Rose Bushes hide behind some trees?

Ⓐ They are scared because Trickster is angry.

Ⓑ They are hiding from hungry Rabbits.

Ⓒ They want to surprise Trickster.

GO ON →

4 Read these sentences from the story.

He thought for a minute about what to do. He decided in just a few *seconds*.

Which word helps you understand what *seconds* means?

Ⓐ thought

Ⓑ minute

Ⓒ decided

5 What is MOST LIKELY the Rose Bushes' point of view at the end of the story?

Ⓐ They are happy to have thorns.

Ⓑ They are scared of the Rabbits.

Ⓒ They are angry with Trickster.

6 What is the lesson of the story?

Ⓐ You should solve problems by yourself.

Ⓑ Rose Bushes can fly on the wind.

Ⓒ It is okay to ask for help.

GO ON →

Read "Nickels" before you answer Numbers 7 through 15.

Nickels

You are in a store. You reach into your pocket. You pull out a nickel. What can you buy? Not much. Can you get a game? You would need to **haul** a heavy bag of nickels for that! Still, the nickel is very interesting.

The first five-cent coin was not called a nickel. Why? Because it was not made of nickel! Like the dime, this coin was made of silver. All U.S. coins used to be made of gold, silver, or copper. It was the law.

The first five-cent coin was called a half dime. It was smaller than our nickel. That is because silver costs more than nickel. The value of silver coins was based on their weight. So the half dime was half the weight of a ten-cent dime.

In 1866, Congress told the U.S. Mint to make a new five-cent coin. It was made of nickel and copper. It was larger. And it was easier to handle than the half dime. This coin was called the nickel.

GO ON →

Nickel is a hard metal. This caused problems for coin makers. Machine parts broke. Workers had to **repair** the parts. So what did they do? They built new machines.

The Mint was making the new nickel. But the half dime was still being made. This presented a problem. Both coins were in use at the same time. What was the solution? The U.S. stopped making the half dime in 1873.

And the nickel we use today? It was first made in 1938. Thomas Jefferson's face is on the front. We all know that a nickel is **worth** five cents. But most people do not know the story behind the coin!

Metals in a Nickel

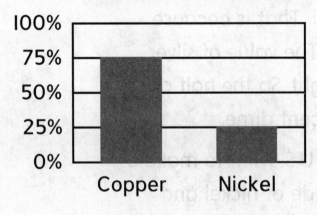

GO ON →

Use "Nickels" to answer Numbers 7 through I5.

7 What clue helps you figure out the author's purpose for writing the article?

Ⓐ The author gives many facts about nickels.

Ⓑ The author asks the reader many questions.

Ⓒ The author tells many funny stories about nickels.

8 Read this sentence from the article.

You would need to *haul* a heavy bag of nickels for that!

Which word helps you understand what *haul* means?

Ⓐ need

Ⓑ heavy

Ⓒ nickels

9 Why was the first five-cent coin called a half dime?

Ⓐ It was made of silver.

Ⓑ It was small and hard to handle.

Ⓒ It was half the weight of a ten-cent dime.

GO ON →

10 What solved the problems caused by nickel being a hard metal?

Ⓐ Workers made half dimes.

Ⓑ Workers built new machines.

Ⓒ Workers stopped making nickels.

11 Read these sentences from the article.

Machine parts broke. Workers had to *repair* the parts.

Which word means the OPPOSITE of *repair*?

Ⓐ broke

Ⓑ parts

Ⓒ workers

12 What problem did the U.S. Mint solve when it stopped making the half dime?

Ⓐ The half dime was much harder to handle than the nickel.

Ⓑ The half dime and nickel were in use at the same time.

Ⓒ The half dime was half the weight of a dime.

GO ON →

13 Read this sentence from the article.

> **Thomas Jefferson's face is on the front. We all know that a nickel is *worth* five cents.**

Which words help explain what *worth* means?

Ⓐ the front

Ⓑ all know

Ⓒ five cents

14 Why did the author MOST LIKELY write this article?

Ⓐ to tell readers the history of the nickel

Ⓑ to let readers know the value of a nickel

Ⓒ to teach readers about Thomas Jefferson

15 Look at the bar graph. How much of a nickel coin is made of copper?

Ⓐ 25%

Ⓑ 75%

Ⓒ 100%

STOP

Exit
Assessment

Read "Kim Gets a Book" before you answer Numbers I through 8.

Kim Gets a Book

Dad took Kim to the book store.

She had some money to **spend**.

Kim wanted to buy an animal book.

Which book would Kim get?

One book had pictures of a lion.

The big cat is **wild**.

It is not tame like Kim's cat.

Kim liked the pictures.

But she does not like lions.

She likes Fluff, her cat.

Fluff plays with Kim.

Fluff is a sweet cat.

Dad found a book.

It had pictures of a brown wolf.

A wolf can howl.

Kim has a brown dog named Ruff.

Ruff can howl, too.

Ruff knows how to fetch.

Ruff is a nice dog.

Ruff is not a wolf!

GO ON →

Kim saw a snake book.

Some snakes have spots.

Some snakes have stripes.

It was fun to look at the snake book.

But Kim does not like snakes.

Kim tried to pick a book.

She liked the lion book.

She liked the wolf book.

She liked the snake book.

Kim liked all the animal books.

Then Kim **peered** around the corner.

She saw another book.

The book had no words or pictures.

It was a large sketch book.

Kim got the sketch book.

Now she can make her own animal book.

Kim can make pictures of Fluff and Ruff!

It is the best book of all!

GO ON →

Name: _____ **Date:** _____

Use "Kim Gets a Book" to answer Numbers 1 through 8.

1 Which word is a clue to what *spend* means?

Ⓐ wanted

Ⓑ some

Ⓒ buy

2 Who takes Kim to the book store?

Ⓐ Kim

Ⓑ Dad

Ⓒ Ruff

3 Who is Fluff?

Ⓐ Kim's cat

Ⓑ Kim's dog

Ⓒ Kim's lion

GO ON →

4 Which word means the OPPOSITE of *wild*?

   Ⓐ shop

   Ⓑ tame

   Ⓒ sweet

5 What can a wolf do?

   Ⓐ A wolf can play.

   Ⓑ A wolf can howl.

   Ⓒ A wolf can fetch.

6 Read these sentences from the story.

   **Then Kim *peered* around the corner.
She saw another book.**

Which word is a clue to what *peered* means?

   Ⓐ around

   Ⓑ corner

   Ⓒ saw

GO ON ➜

Name: _____ **Date:** _____

7 Which book does Kim like best?

   Ⓐ the sketch book

   Ⓑ the snake book

   Ⓒ the wolf book

8 What can Kim make?

   Ⓐ a book store

   Ⓑ pictures of Dad

   Ⓒ her own animal book

Read "Video Pals" before you answer Numbers 9 through 15.

Video Pals

Luke lives in Texas.

His pal Ben lives in Canada.

The pals have a nice **friendship**.

Luke wants to know more about Ben.

Ben wants to know more about Luke.

What does Luke eat?

What sports does Ben like?

Luke and Ben make videos.

Luke plans a lunch.

It is at his ranch.

Dad makes stew.

Mom makes corn.

Luke and Mom make a cake.

It is the shape of Texas.

Ben likes the video.

He thinks the lunch looks tasty!

GO ON →

Then Ben plans a lunch.

It is at the lake.

Dad grills fish.

Mom makes a salad.

Ben and Dad make maple leaf candy.

Luke likes the video.

He thinks the lunch looks yummy!

Next Luke makes a sports video.

Luke likes baseball.

The Reds play the Cubs.

Six Cubs make home runs!

Luke cheers for the Cubs!

Ben makes a sports video.

Ben likes hockey.

The Flames play the Jets.

One Jet scores five goals!

Ben cheers for the Jets!

It was fun to make the videos.

It was fun to watch them!

Now the boys will be better friends.

Ben has **invited** Luke to visit him.

He has asked Luke to come to Canada.

Ben and Luke will have a great time!

GO ON →

Use "Video Pen Pals" to answer Numbers 9 through 15.

9 Which clue tells what *friendship* means?

Ⓐ Luke

Ⓑ pals

Ⓒ nice

10 How do the boys get to know each other?

Ⓐ They make videos.

Ⓑ They make a cake.

Ⓒ They make home runs.

11 Where does Luke live?

Ⓐ in Texas

Ⓑ with Ben

Ⓒ at the lake

12 What does Ben's family make for lunch?

Ⓐ stew, corn, cake

Ⓑ chili, bread, pie

Ⓒ fish, salad, candy

GO ON →

13 Which sports team does Luke like?

Ⓐ Reds

Ⓑ Cubs

Ⓒ Flames

14 What is Ben's favorite sport?

Ⓐ hockey

Ⓑ playing

Ⓒ baseball

15 Read these sentences from the article.

Ben has *invited* Luke to visit him.
He has asked Luke to come to Canada.

Which word means the SAME as *invited*?

Ⓐ visit

Ⓑ asked

Ⓒ come

STOP

Read "Three Baby Turtles" before you answer Numbers 1 through 7.

Three Baby Turtles

Brian was riding in the car with his mom. It was afternoon. They were driving down the dirt road.

"Stop the car!" cried Brian. His mom stopped the car.

"What is it?" she asked. Brian jumped out of the car. He went to the side of the road.

"Baby turtles!" he said. There were three baby turtles. They were crawling in the dirt.

"Oh, they look weak," said Mom. "I don't see a mother turtle. They need some help."

"Then we should help them," said Brian. His mom agreed. Brian put the turtles in a shoebox. They drove home.

Later, Brian and his mom drove to Betsy's Pet Store. They got a big glass tank. This would be the turtles' home.

GO ON →

"You have to keep the water **fresh**," said Betsy.

"That means new water every day or so," said Mom.

They got a heat lamp for the tank. They also got pet food made just for turtles. They had everything they needed to take care of the turtles.

Every day Brian fed the turtles and changed the turtles' water. He kept the tank clean. After a few weeks, the turtles were healthy. They began to grow.

"Way to go, Brian," said Mom. "You saved those turtles! Now they can grow old. They will be **alive** for many years."

That made Brian feel pretty good.

GO ON →

Name: _____ **Date:** _____

Use "Three Baby Turtles" to answer Numbers 1 through 7.

1 What are Brian and his mother doing at the BEGINNING of the story?

Ⓐ crawling in the dirt

Ⓑ going to the pet store

Ⓒ driving down a dirt road

2 Why does Brian jump out of the car?

Ⓐ He is with Mom.

Ⓑ He sees baby turtles.

Ⓒ He likes to jump in the road.

3 What problem do the turtles have?

Ⓐ They look weak and need help.

Ⓑ They are crawling in the dirt.

Ⓒ They live with Brian.

4 Which sentence from the story tells why Brian gets a tank?

Ⓐ His mom agreed.

Ⓑ This would be the turtles' home.

Ⓒ They got a heat lamp for the tank.

GO ON →

Exit Assessment · Unit 2   Grade 2   **189**

5 Which sentence from the story helps you know what *fresh* means?

Ⓐ "Oh, they look weak," said Mom.

Ⓑ "Then we should help them," said Brian.

Ⓒ "That means new water every day or so," said Mom.

6 How does Brian solve the turtles' problem?

Ⓐ Brian feeds and cares for the turtles.

Ⓑ Brian puts the turtles in a shoebox.

Ⓒ Brian gets a mother turtle.

7 Read these sentences from the story.

"Way to go, Brian," said Mom. "You saved those turtles! Now they can grow old. They will be *alive* for many years."

Which words help explain what *alive* means?

Ⓐ way to go

Ⓑ those turtles

Ⓒ can grow old

**Read "Big Owl's Big Night" before you answer
Numbers 8 through 15.**

Big Owl's Big Night

The sun is going down. In the forest, most animals
are going to sleep. Not Big Owl! Big Owl is a Great
Horned Owl. His night has only begun!

Owls like the night. Hunters cannot see an owl's
wings **flapping**, or moving up and down.

Big Owl wakes up in his nest. Like other owls, his
nest is in a hole in a tree.

He steps onto a branch. He begins to sing. Owls
use their voices to call to other owls. Big Owl hoots.
"I am here!" he is saying. He listens. Others owls
hoot back.

Great Horned Owl

Ear tufts

Dark ring
around face

Talons

GO ON →

It is getting very dark out. It is time to eat. Owls like to **feast** on mice. Big Owl sits on a branch. He looks below. His eyes are sharp. He can see in the dark. Soon enough, he **spies** a mouse! He sees it running. Big Owl swoops down. He uses his large talons, or claws, to grab his dinner.

Hours later, the sun comes up. It is too light out for Big Owl. Crows may be near. Crows like to bother Big Owl. It is time for bed. Big Owl flies back to his tree. He climbs into his hole. He falls asleep.

GO ON →

Use "Big Owl's Big Night" to answer Numbers 8 through 15.

8 What is the MAIN topic of the article?

Ⓐ when most animals go to sleep

Ⓑ where owls make their nests

Ⓒ what owls do at night

9 Why do owls like the night?

Ⓐ Hunters cannot see their wings.

Ⓑ It is a good time to sleep.

Ⓒ They can stay in a hole.

10 Which words from the aricle tell what *flapping* means?

Ⓐ an owl's wings

Ⓑ wakes up in his nest

Ⓒ moving up and down

GO ON →

Name: _____ Date: _____

11 What is a key detail about some owls' nests?

Ⓐ The nests are in the holes of trees.

Ⓑ The nests are where owls eat their meals.

Ⓒ The nests are good places for owls to sing.

12 What do owls use their voices for?

Ⓐ to call to other owls

Ⓑ to find their dinner

Ⓒ to bother crows

13 Look at the diagram on page 191. Which body part gives the Great Horned Owl its name?

Ⓐ dark ring

Ⓑ ear tufts

Ⓒ talons

GO ON →

14 Read these sentences from the article.

> **It is getting very dark out. It is time to eat. Owls like to *feast* on mice. Big Owl sits on a branch. He looks below.**

Which words help you know what *feast* means?

Ⓐ very dark out

Ⓑ time to eat

Ⓒ looks below

15 Read these sentences from the article.

> **Soon enough, he *spies* a mouse! He sees it running. Big Owl swoops down.**

Which words mean about the SAME as *spies*?

Ⓐ sees it running

Ⓑ swoops down

Ⓒ soon enough

STOP

Read "The Mural" before you answer Numbers I through 8.

The Mural

"All right, class," Mr. Smith said. "Please sit down."

The school mural contest was about to take place. Each year, Mr. Smith chose one design. Then a new mural was painted in the hallway.

"I'm going to win," Liz said. "I can feel it." Liz **enjoyed** painting. It was her favorite thing to do.

"Sorry," Mike said. "This is my year." Mike loved to draw. He always drew shapes in his notebook.

The next day, Mike was sitting on a bench in the playground. He was working on his design. Liz walked over and sat down next to him.

"Hey, Mike," Liz said. "Can I **borrow** a black marker?"

"Sure. I'll lend you a marker if you let me see your design. Deal?"

"Deal," replied Liz. Then she opened her sketch book to reveal her desert scene.

"Wow!" Mike cried. "Your sand is pink! And that cactus is blue! That is so cool."

GO ON →

"Let me see your design," Liz said. Mike opened his notebook. The page was filled with ovals, lines, and dots. Liz had never seen anything like it. She closed her book.

"Your design is better than mine," she said. "I don't think I'll enter the contest this year."

"My design is good," Mike said. "But your colors are better. I have an idea. Let's use my design and your colors. Let's enter the contest together."

One week later, Mike and Liz stood in front of their new mural. They both smiled as their classmates clapped and **cheered**.

Use "The Mural" to answer Numbers I through 8.

1 What happens FIRST in the story?

&Ⓐ Mr. Smith asks the class to sit down.

Ⓑ Mike sits on a playground bench.

Ⓒ Liz opens her sketch book.

2 Which sentence from the story helps explain what *enjoyed* means?

Ⓐ Each year, Mr. Smith chose one design.

Ⓑ It was her favorite thing to do.

Ⓒ Mike opened his notebook.

3 What happens right AFTER Liz says she is going to win the contest?

Ⓐ The mural contest ends.

Ⓑ Mr. Smith's class sits down.

Ⓒ Mike says it is his year to win.

4 Which word is a clue to what *borrow* means?

Ⓐ said

Ⓑ lend

Ⓒ see

5 What happens AFTER Mike lends Liz a marker?

Ⓐ Liz starts to draw her design.

Ⓑ Liz sits next to Mike on the bench.

Ⓒ Liz reveals her desert scene to Mike.

GO ON →

6 What happens BEFORE Mike says he and Liz should enter the contest together?

Ⓐ Mike says Liz's colors are better than his.

Ⓑ Mike says Liz's design is better than his.

Ⓒ Mike and Liz smile at their classmates.

7 Why do Liz and Mike stand in front of their new mural at the END of the story?

Ⓐ They decided not to enter the contest.

Ⓑ They are the winners of the contest.

Ⓒ They did not win the contest.

8 Read this sentence from the story.

They both smiled as their classmates clapped and *cheered*.

Which word means about the SAME as *cheered*?

Ⓐ smiled

Ⓑ classmates

Ⓒ clapped

GO ON →

Read "Volcanoes" before you answer Numbers 9 through 15.

Volcanoes

Volcanoes are mountains with an opening at the top. Liquid rock is under a volcano. Pressure builds inside. The pressure can get high. Then the volcano erupts. Liquid rock shoots out of the opening. The liquid rock flows out. It flows down the mountain. Gas shoots out. The gas fills the air. Hot volcanic ash covers the ground.

Bad things can happen when volcanoes erupt. Ash and liquid rock **damage** homes. They harm animals and plants. They knock down forests.

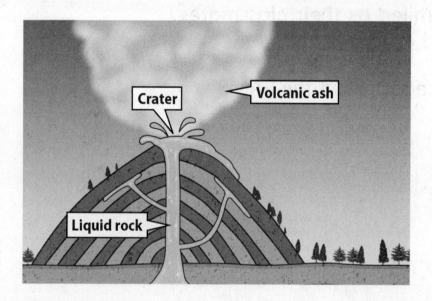

Crater

Volcanic ash

Liquid rock

GO ON →

Good things can happen when volcanoes erupt, too. Are you surprised?

Volcanic ash improves the soil. It is full of minerals. Liquid rock cools and breaks down. This also helps the soil. Farms near volcanoes do well. They produce lots of vegetables.

Underground water near volcanoes gets very hot. People drill wells. The water comes out as steam. This steam is used to make electricity. Then the steam cools. It becomes hot water again. This water can heat homes.

Volcanoes attract visitors. Some volcanoes create **amazing** geysers. Tourists wonder at the water shooting up. What a great show!

GO ON →

Name: _____ Date: _____

Use "Volcanoes" to answer Numbers 9 through 15.

9 What happens when a volcano erupts?

Ⓐ Hot ash shoots into the mountain.

Ⓑ Liquid rock flows down the mountain.

Ⓒ The mountain has an opening at the top.

10 Read these sentences from the article.

Bad things can happen when volcanoes erupt. Ash and liquid rock *damage* homes. They harm animals and plants.

Which word tells you what *damage* means?

Ⓐ erupt

Ⓑ liquid

Ⓒ harm

11 Why did the author include a diagram in the article?

Ⓐ to add more details about volcanoes

Ⓑ to show good things volcanoes do

Ⓒ to make the article look nicer

12 Look at the diagram on page 200. What is the opening at the top of a volcano called?

Ⓐ volcanic ash

Ⓑ liquid rock

Ⓒ crater

13 Which sentence from the article supports the idea that volcanoes improve the soil?

Ⓐ Farms near volcanoes do well.

Ⓑ The water comes out as steam.

Ⓒ Liquid rock cools and breaks down.

GO ON →

14 Read these sentences from the article.

Some volcanoes create *amazing* geysers. Tourists wonder at the water shooting up.

Which clue word helps explain what *amazing* means?

Ⓐ geysers

Ⓑ wonder

Ⓒ shooting

15 Why did the author MOST LIKELY write this article?

Ⓐ to tell a story about how volcanoes erupt

Ⓑ to give reasons why tourists like volcanoes

Ⓒ to explain why volcanoes are bad and good

STOP

Read "Two Big Lakes" before you answer Numbers I through 8.

Two Big Lakes

Lakes are all over the country. But not all lakes are alike. Crater Lake and Great Salt Lake are famous lakes. Crater Lake is in Oregon. Great Salt Lake is in Utah. People love to see these lakes. They travel from all over.

How They Formed

The two lakes were formed in different ways. A volcano erupted 7,000 years ago. This caused a hole in the **earth**, or ground. Rainwater filled the hole. This became Crater Lake.

Great Salt Lake formed from an older lake. This old lake was huge! It was ten times bigger than Great Salt Lake. The old lake shrank. Great Salt Lake is what was left.

One Salty, One Fresh

The water in Great Salt Lake is salty. Rivers bring small amounts of salt to the lake. However, the water cannot flow to the sea. The salt stays in the lake. Great Salt Lake is too salty for fish. There are no fish in Great Salt Lake.

GO ON →

The water in Crater Lake is fresh. It is not salty. There are fish in Crater Lake. People put them there so they could go fishing.

Fun for Everyone

Both lakes get **plenty** of visitors. Lots of people go to see them.

The lakes are pretty. Crater Lake has very blue water. It is as blue as the sky. Mountains are all around Crater Lake. People hike in the mountains. At Great Salt Lake, people play on the shore. They play in the sand.

You should go to one of these places. Each **location** is very interesting.

Use "Two Big Lakes" to answer Numbers 1 through 8.

1 Read these sentences from the article.

This caused a hole in the *earth*, or ground. Rainwater filled the hole.

Which word means the SAME as *earth*?

Ⓐ filled

Ⓑ caused

Ⓒ ground

GO ON →

2 What caused Crater Lake to form?

Ⓐ a volcano erupted

Ⓑ an older lake shrank

Ⓒ a river flowed to the sea

3 Why are there no fish in Great Salt Lake?

Ⓐ The water cannot flow to the sea.

Ⓑ The water is as blue as the sky.

Ⓒ The water has too much salt.

4 How are the two lakes DIFFERENT?

Ⓐ One has salt water and one has fresh water.

Ⓑ One is in Oregon and one is in a crater.

Ⓒ One is pretty and one is not.

5 How are the two lakes ALIKE?

Ⓐ Both lakes are in Utah.

Ⓑ Both lakes get lots of visitors.

Ⓒ Both lakes were formed by older lakes.

GO ON →

6 Which word from the article means almost the SAME as *plenty*?

Ⓐ lots

Ⓑ very

Ⓒ pretty

7 Which subheading would you use to find out about things to do at the lakes?

Ⓐ How They Formed

Ⓑ One Salty, One Fresh

Ⓒ Fun for Everyone

8 Read these sentences from the article.

You should go to one of these places. Each *location* is very interesting.

Which word means about the SAME as *location*?

Ⓐ places

Ⓑ should

Ⓒ these

Read "Raj and Me" before you answer Numbers 9 through 15.

Raj and Me

"Okay, class," said Ms. Lewis. "Today we will be working on a project. You and your partner will create a report. It will be about a holiday you celebrate."

I was happy. These kinds of projects always **excite** my interest.

"Luis," she said to me. "You will be working with Raj."

This worried me. It wasn't that I did not like Raj. I did. But Raj had just moved here from India. My family and I come from Mexico. I did not think we would have very much in common.

"What should we do our report about?" I asked.

"I don't know much about American holidays," said Raj.

"Hmm," I said. "Well, what holidays does your family celebrate?"

"We celebrate India's Day of Freedom," said Raj.

"My family celebrates a Mexican Day of Freedom," I said.

GO ON →

Raj and I talked about the two holidays. Both holidays celebrate freedom. India became free from Great Britain in 1947. Mexico became free from Spain in 1821.

"My favorite part is the food we eat," said Raj. "My parents cook up a big feast!"

"We have a feast, too," I said. "But my favorite part is the **parades.** There are bands. There are lots of people marching around the block."

"They have parades in India, too," said Raj.

We decided to do our report on both of our holidays. Ms. Lewis loved it. So did the rest of the class. I was glad Raj was my partner!

GO ON →

Use "Raj and Me" to answer Numbers 9 through 15.

9 Read these sentences from the story.

I was happy. These kinds of projects always *excite* my interest.

Which word gives you a clue about what *excite* means?

Ⓐ happy

Ⓑ always

Ⓒ projects

10 Why is Luis worried about having Raj as his partner?

Ⓐ He thinks Raj will do all the work.

Ⓑ He thinks the project will be too easy.

Ⓒ He thinks they do not have a lot in common.

11 How is Raj DIFFERENT from Luis?

Ⓐ Raj celebrates a Day of Freedom.

Ⓑ Raj is from India and Luis is from Mexico.

Ⓒ Luis wants to report on American holidays.

GO ON ➜

12 How are Raj and Luis ALIKE?

Ⓐ They are in the same class.

Ⓑ They come from the same place.

Ⓒ They both like to march in parades.

13 Read these sentences from the story.

"But my favorite part is the *parades*. There are bands. There are lots of people marching around the block."

Which words help you understand what *parades* means?

Ⓐ favorite part

Ⓑ people marching

Ⓒ around the block

GO ON →

14 What happens when Luis and Raj work together on the project?

Ⓐ They learn more about each other.

Ⓑ They write about one holiday.

Ⓒ They become best friends.

15 What is the theme of this story?

Ⓐ People from India and Mexico have freedom holidays.

Ⓑ People from different places can be alike in many ways.

Ⓒ People do better when they work on projects by themselves.

STOP

Read "Saving the Birds" before you answer Numbers I through 8.

Saving the Birds

Boyd attends the first meeting of the nature club. The advisor asks students to think of ways to help animals. Boyd thinks about his brother.

Boyd's brother is much older. His name is Jack. He studies biology at school. He plans to become a veterinarian.

Jack is one of Boyd's heroes. He brags about Jack all the time. Jack feels strongly about the environment. He wants to protect Earth's **resources**. This includes all things found in nature that people can use.

Years ago, Jack helped clean a beach after an oil spill. Jack passed many birds on the beach. They were covered in oil. They could not fly away. He wanted to help them.

Jack **volunteered**, or offered his time, to help the birds. He worked with a bird rescue center. He learned how to clean birds with a mild soap. The birds were fed. Then they swam in small pools. They stayed at the center for weeks.

GO ON →

Boyd calls Jack. He tells him about the nature club. He asks if he can go to the rescue center. He wants to take care of the birds.

Jack says Boyd is too young. He will not be able to care for the birds. He has to learn about them first. Then he can clean their cages.

Jack takes Boyd to the center. Two birds have been hurt by an oil spill. Jack is **patient** with them. He calmly waits for them to relax. He tells Boyd the birds are scared. Jack gently washes the birds. He cleans their feathers with soap. Later, Boyd helps Jack feed the birds. He cleans their cages.

Jack says the birds will live. Boyd is happy he helped them. Boyd will talk to the nature club about his bird rescue work.

Use "Saving the Birds" to answer Numbers I through 8.

1 How does Boyd show what he thinks of Jack?

Ⓐ Boyd attends a nature club meeting.

Ⓑ Boyd brags about Jack all the time.

Ⓒ Boyd thinks Jack is much older.

GO ON →

Name: _____ **Date:** _____

2 Read these sentences from the story.

> He wants to protect Earth's *resources.*
> This includes all things found in nature
> that people can use.

Which words help you understand what
resources means?

Ⓐ people can use

Ⓑ wants to protect

Ⓒ things found in nature

3 What problem does the oil spill cause?

Ⓐ The birds are covered in oil.

Ⓑ The birds do not need any help.

Ⓒ The birds fly away from the spill.

4 Which word from the story means about the
SAME as *volunteered*?

Ⓐ passed

Ⓑ wanted

Ⓒ offered

5 How does Jack help solve the birds' problem?

Ⓐ He is Boyd's older brother.

Ⓑ He sees the oil spill on the beach.

Ⓒ He helps clean the birds' feathers.

6 What is Boyd's problem?

Ⓐ Jack says he is too young.

Ⓑ Jack says the birds will live.

Ⓒ Jack is one of Boyd's heroes.

7 What is Boyd's point of view about working with Jack at the rescue?

Ⓐ He is happy because he helped the birds.

Ⓑ He could not clean the oil from the birds.

Ⓒ He wants to be a veterinarian like Jack.

8 Which sentence from the story helps explain what *patient* means?

Ⓐ They stayed at the center for weeks.

Ⓑ He calmly waits for them to relax.

Ⓒ Jack says the birds will live.

GO ON ➔

Read "Rules for Being Active" before you
answer Numbers 9 through 15.

Rules for Being Active

Most states require schools to have physical
education classes, but not all do. As the U.S.
government focuses more on health and nutrition,
states may have kids spending more time in
the gym.

Why is being active important? Active kids have
more energy. They do not get sick so easily. They
are more alert.

Kids do not have to go to school to be active.
They can jog. They can do yoga. They can meet
friends in the park. They can **form,** or make, a
soccer team.

There are many ways to exercise. Health
and fitness Web sites provide rules for getting
started safely.

Start with small changes. Stop if you feel pain.
Have you been sick? Do you have an injury? See a
doctor first.

Kids should exercise for an hour at least
five days a week. Adults should exercise for
30 minutes daily.

GO ON →

Here are three kinds of exercises everyone should do. The first exercise makes the heart beat faster. It includes running. The second one builds strength. It includes curls and lunges. The third kind involves doing stretches.

Wear clothes that are right for the gym or park. Buy shoes that give you support.

Drink water. You do not have to be thirsty.

Stretch for five to 10 minutes after exercising. Hold each stretch for 20 to 30 seconds. Stretching prevents injuries.

Try to be more active right now. Add extra steps to each task. Take the stairs, not the elevator. Do an extra chore at home. Walk around the block as you talk on the phone. Slowly work toward **challenging,** or difficult, tasks.

It is easy to be active and have fun. Just follow these simple rules.

Rules for Exercising	Reason
Drink water	Stay hydrated
Wear the right shoes	Prevent injury
Stretch muscles	Prevent soreness and injury

GO ON →

Use "Rules for Being Active" to answer Numbers 9 through 15.

9 What may be a result of the U.S. government focusing more on health and nutrition?

Ⓐ Some states may require physical education classes in school.

Ⓑ States may have kids spending more time in the gym.

Ⓒ Kids may have to learn three different exercises.

10 What is one thing that happens when kids become more active?

Ⓐ They have more energy.

Ⓑ They do not have to go to school.

Ⓒ They can meet friends on a team.

11 Read these sentences from the article:

> They can meet friends in the park.
> They can *form,* or make, a soccer team.

Which word means about the SAME as *form*?

Ⓐ meet

Ⓑ make

Ⓒ team

12 What is the FIRST thing to do to get ready to exercise safely?

Ⓐ Wait for an adult.

Ⓑ Exercise for an hour.

Ⓒ Start with small changes.

13 What should you do right AFTER exercising?

Ⓐ Stretch for five to 10 minutes.

Ⓑ Walk around the block.

Ⓒ Wear the right clothes.

GO ON →

Name: _____ Date: _____

14 Look at the chart. Why should you wear the right shoes when you exercise?

Ⓐ to stretch muscles

Ⓑ to prevent injury

Ⓒ to stay hydrated

15 Read this sentence from the article.

Slowly work toward *challenging*, or difficult, tasks.

Which word helps you understand what *challenging* means?

Ⓐ work

Ⓑ toward

Ⓒ difficult

STOP

Read "Sun Power" before you answer Numbers I through 9.

Sun Power

We have plenty of energy. We heat our homes with oil. We run our cars on gas. But gas and oil will run out. We need other resources. **Solar** power is a good choice. It comes from the Sun.

People have used the Sun's heat for thousands of years. They built homes to catch sunlight during the winter. In the 1830s, a British scientist **invented** a solar collector. He made the device to cook food. Today, we can use the Sun's power for many things.

We use solar power two ways. One way is as a heat source. Solar power can be changed to heat. Then it is used to heat water. It is used to heat school rooms.

The second way is as an energy source. Electricity is formed using solar panels. The panels take the energy from sunlight. They turn it into electricity. Have you seen highway signs with flashing messages? Solar panels are on those signs. You can see solar panels on top of houses, too.

GO ON →

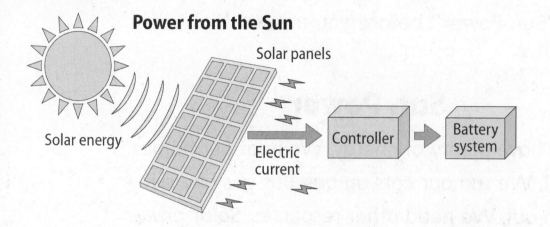

Power from the Sun

Solar panels

Solar energy

Electric current

Controller

Battery system

Solar panels are not harmful. Solar power does not pollute the air. But this resource is not perfect. The amount of sunlight we get does not stay the same. It depends on the time of day and year. It changes with the weather. One place does not get that much energy from the Sun at any one time. So a large area is needed to collect the energy.

Like oil and gas, solar energy can be used as power. Solar power can be used to cook food. It can run **machines** like laptops. It can power cars. It is free. And it will never run out.

GO ON →

Name: _____ Date: _____

Use "Sun Power" to answer Numbers 1 through 9.

1 What is the problem with gas and oil?

Ⓐ They heat our homes.

Ⓑ They are resources.

Ⓒ They will run out.

2 Which words from the article tell you what *solar* means?

Ⓐ plenty of energy

Ⓑ heat our homes

Ⓒ from the Sun

3 Read these sentences from the article.

In the 1830s, a British scientist *invented* a solar collector. He made the device to cook food.

Which words help you understand what the scientist *invented*?

Ⓐ in the 1930s

Ⓑ a solar collector

Ⓒ made the device

GO ON →

4 Why is solar power an important resource?

Ⓐ It is a source of heat and energy.

Ⓑ It makes solar panels for homes.

Ⓒ It depends on the weather.

5 What is the purpose of the diagram in the article?

Ⓐ to tell how to use solar heat

Ⓑ to explain how solar panels work

Ⓒ to show how much solar energy costs

6 Look at the diagram. Where does electric current go AFTER it leaves the controller?

Ⓐ the Sun

Ⓑ solar panels

Ⓒ battery system

Name: _____ Date: _____

7 Which sentence from the article is a MAIN idea about solar power?

Ⓐ The amount of sunlight we get does not stay the same.

Ⓑ Like oil and gas, solar energy can be used as power.

Ⓒ You can see solar panels on top of houses, too.

8 Read these sentences from the article.

Solar power can be used to cook food. It can run *machines* like laptops.

Which word means about the SAME as *machines*?

Ⓐ cook

Ⓑ power

Ⓒ laptops

9 Why did the author write this article?

Ⓐ to teach readers about solar power

Ⓑ to show readers how to build solar panels

Ⓒ to tell readers about the first solar collector

Copyright © McGraw-Hill Education. Permission is granted to reproduce for classroom use.

GO ON →

Exit Assessment · Unit 6   Grade 2   **227**

Read "Why Turkey Gobbles" before you answer Numbers 10 through 15.

Why Turkey Gobbles

Long ago, the animals played many games. The birds liked to play ball games. They shouted just as players do today. Some yelled better than others.

Grouse had a good voice. He could shout loudly at the ball game. "Let's go team!" he would shout. But Turkey could not shout. Turkey could make no noise at all.

One day, Turkey talked to Grouse after a game. "Will you teach me how to use my voice?" Turkey asked. "Will you give me lessons?"

"Of course I will," Grouse said. "But I want something in return." Grouse looked at Turkey for a minute. "I like your **dazzling** black feathers," he said. "They are so bright. Will you give me some of your feathers? Then I can make a collar for my neck."

"You want my feathers?" Turkey asked. "Well, I guess that would be fair." So Turkey plucked some of his finest feathers. He gave them to Grouse. That is how Grouse got his collar of feathers.

GO ON →

They began the voice lessons. Turkey was a fast learner. Soon Grouse thought Turkey was ready. It was time to try Turkey's voice at a distance. He wanted to see how far Turkey could shout.

"Please go stand by those **crops** of corn," Grouse said. "I will stand here. I will give the signal by tapping on this tree. Then you shout as loudly as you can."

Turkey was eager and excited. Grouse gave the signal. Turkey tried to shout. He tried again. But he could not raise his voice. All he could say was, "Gobble! Gobble! Gobble!"

Ever since that day, whenever Turkey hears a noise, he can only gobble.

GO ON →

Use "Why Turkey Gobbles" to answer Numbers 10 through 15.

10 What is Turkey's point of view about Grouse at the BEGINNING of the story?

Ⓐ Grouse would be a good voice teacher.

Ⓑ Grouse is good at playing ball games.

Ⓒ Grouse cannot make any noise at all.

11 Read these sentences from the story.

"I like your *dazzling* black feathers," he said. "They are so bright."

Which word means about the SAME as *dazzling*?

Ⓐ black

Ⓑ bright

Ⓒ feathers

12 Why does Turkey think it is fair to give Grouse some feathers?

Ⓐ Grouse will give Turkey some feathers.

Ⓑ Grouse will give Turkey voice lessons.

Ⓒ Grouse will give Turkey a signal.

GO ON →

13 Read this sentence from the story.

> **"Please go stand by those *crops* of corn,"
> Grouse said.**

Which word helps explain what *crops* means?

Ⓐ stand

Ⓑ those

Ⓒ corn

14 Which sentence BEST supports the lesson of the story?

Ⓐ Soon Grouse thought Turkey was ready.

Ⓑ But he could not raise his voice.

Ⓒ Turkey was a fast learner.

15 What is the lesson of the story?

Ⓐ Things do not always work out the way we hope they will.

Ⓑ It is good to give something in return for lessons.

Ⓒ Animals do not make good teachers.

STOP

Fluency
Assessment

Jazz

My name is Phillip. This is my pet hamster Jazz.

He is brown with spots of white.

He has a little pink nose.

He is small and very cute.

This is his cage. It is where he plays and sleeps.

He sleeps most of the day. He plays at night.

There is a wheel in his cage. Jazz likes to run.

He goes up on the wheel.

He goes down on the wheel.

Then Jazz drinks some water and eats.

I change his water and food every day.

Jazz is the best.

✓ Who is Jazz?

✓ What does the narrator think of Jazz?

Name: _____ Date: _____

Jazz

10	My name is Phillip. This is my pet hamster Jazz.
17	He is brown with spots of white.
23	He has a little pink nose.
29	He is small and very cute.
40	This is his cage. It is where he plays and sleeps.
50	He sleeps most of the day. He plays at night.
61	There is a wheel in his cage. Jazz likes to run.
67	He goes up on the wheel.
73	He goes down on the wheel.
80	Then Jazz drinks some water and eats.
88	I change his water and food every day.
92	Jazz is the best.

 Who is Jazz?

 What does the narrator think of Jazz?

Words Read	-	Errors	=	WCPM

☐ **Fall (51 WCPM)**
☐ **Winter (72 WCPM)**
☐ **Spring (89 WCPM)**

WCPM	÷	Words Read	=	Accuracy %

PROSODY	L1	L2	L3	L4
Reading in Phrases	O	O	O	O
Pace	O	O	O	O
Syntax	O	O	O	O
Self-correction	O	O	O	O
Intonation	O	O	O	O

So Many Ants

There are many kinds of ants.

Most ants are small.

But some are big. Ants can be one inch long.

Most ants are black.

There are yellow and green ants too.

There are even purple ants.

Some ants live in trees.

Others make nests in sand.

Ants are strong. They can lift big things.

They can lift things that are bigger than them!

Ants help each other. Some ants make nests.

Other ants protect the nests.

A different group looks for food.

There is another important job.

It is to care for baby ants.

Look for ants in a park. They are fun to watch!

✔ What is the MAIN idea of the article?

✔ How do ants help each other?

Name: _____   Date: _____

So Many Ants

6	There are many kinds of ants.
10	Most ants are small.
20	But some are big. Ants can be one inch long.
24	Most ants are black.
31	There are yellow and green ants too.
36	There are even purple ants.
41	Some ants live in trees.
46	Others make nests in sand.
54	Ants are strong. They can lift big things.
63	They can lift things that are bigger than them!
71	Ants help each other. Some ants make nests.
76	Other ants protect the nests.
82	A different group looks for food.
87	There is another important job.
94	It is to care for baby ants.
105	Look for ants in a park. They are fun to watch!

✔ What is the MAIN idea of the article?

✔ How do ants help each other?

Words Read	-	Errors	=	WCPM

☐ **Fall (51 WCPM)**
☐ **Winter (72 WCPM)**
☐ **Spring (89 WCPM)**

WCPM	÷	Words Read	=	Accuracy %

PROSODY				
	L1	L2	L3	L4
Reading in Phrases	O	O	O	O
Pace	O	O	O	O
Syntax	O	O	O	O
Self-correction	O	O	O	O
Intonation	O	O	O	O

Elephant and Turtle

Elephant sat up and looked at the clock.

He would be late for school!

Elephant got dressed. He ate a banana.

He grabbed his books.

He put them in a backpack.

Elephant ran down the street.

He had to get to school!

On the way, he saw Turtle.

Turtle was also late for school.

Turtle walked very slowly.

Elephant knew that Turtle would be very late.

He knew that Turtle would get in trouble.

So Elephant had an idea.

He put Turtle in his backpack.

Elephant ran all the way to school.

They got to class before the bell rang.

They were not late.

👆 How does Elephant help Turtle?

👆 What is the message of this story?

Name: _____   Date: _____

Elephant and Turtle

8	Elephant sat up and looked at the clock.
14	He would be late for school!
21	Elephant got dressed. He ate a banana.
25	He grabbed his books.
31	He put them in a backpack.
36	Elephant ran down the street.
42	He had to get to school!
48	On the way, he saw Turtle.
54	Turtle was also late for school.
58	Turtle walked very slowly.
66	Elephant knew that Turtle would be very late.
74	He knew that Turtle would get in trouble.
79	So Elephant had an idea.
85	He put Turtle in his backpack.
92	Elephant ran all the way to school.
100	They got to class before the bell rang.
104	They were not late.

How does Elephant help Turtle?

What is the message of this story?

Words Read	-	Errors	=	WCPM

☐ **Fall (51 WCPM)**
☐ **Winter (72 WCPM)**
☐ **Spring (89 WCPM)**

WCPM	÷	Words Read	=	Accuracy %

PROSODY				
	L1	L2	L3	L4
Reading in Phrases	O	O	O	O
Pace	O	O	O	O
Syntax	O	O	O	O
Self-correction	O	O	O	O
Intonation	O	O	O	O

Bird Homes

Where do birds live? Birds live in many places.

This bird lives in a park. It hops in the grass.

It picks up twigs with its beak.

The bird uses twigs to make a nest.

Look into the nest. What do you see?

You may see eggs. You may see baby birds.

This bird lives in the woods.

Do you hear that sound?

The bird is pecking a hole in a tree. It is loud.

His beak is strong to peck a hole.

It cuts a hole in the tree for a home.

✓ What do birds use to make a nest?

✓ Why does a bird make a hole in a tree?

Name: _____ Date: _____

Bird Homes

9	Where do birds live? Birds live in many places.
20	This bird lives in a park. It hops in the grass.
27	It picks up twigs with its beak.
35	The bird uses twigs to make a nest.
43	Look into the nest. What do you see?
52	You may see eggs. You may see baby birds.
58	This bird lives in the woods.
63	Do you hear that sound?
75	The bird is pecking a hole in a tree. It is loud.
83	His beak is strong to peck a hole.
93	It cuts a hole in the tree for a home.

✔ What do birds use to make a nest?

✔ Why does a bird make a hole in a tree?

Words Read	-	Errors	=	WCPM

☐ **Fall (51 WCPM)**
☐ **Winter (72 WCPM)**
☐ **Spring (89 WCPM)**

WCPM	÷	Words Read	=	Accuracy %

PROSODY	L1	L2	L3	L4
Reading in Phrases	O	O	O	O
Pace	O	O	O	O
Syntax	O	O	O	O
Self-correction	O	O	O	O
Intonation	O	O	O	O

Crab and Clam

One day, Crab saw Clam on the beach.

He said, "You are like me."

Crab had a shell. Clam had one, too.

Clam said, "Yes, and we both live near the sea."

Crab had many strong legs.

He could run very fast.

He said, "Can you run, Clam?"

"No," said Clam. He was slow.

Clam had one foot.

He used it to get around. It could scoop sand.

Clam ate plants.

He asked, "What do you eat, Crab?"

"I eat clams!" said Crab.

Crab didn't look so friendly anymore.

Clam moved as fast as he could.

"Bye!" yelled Clam.

☑ How are Clam and Crab alike?

☑ Why does Clam leave at the end of the story?

Name: _____ Date: _____

Crab and Clam

8	One day, Crab saw Clam on the beach.
14	He said, "You are like me."
22	Crab had a shell. Clam had one, too.
32	Clam said, "Yes, and we both live near the sea."
37	Crab had many strong legs.
42	He could run very fast.
48	He said, "Can you run, Clam?"
54	"No," said Clam. He was slow.
58	Clam had one foot.
68	He used it to get around. It could scoop sand.
71	Clam ate plants.
78	He asked, "What do you eat, Crab?"
83	"I eat clams!" said Crab.
89	Crab didn't look so friendly anymore.
96	Clam moved as fast as he could.
99	"Bye!" yelled Clam.

✔ How are Clam and Crab alike?

✔ Why does Clam leave at the end of the story?

Words Read	-	Errors	=	WCPM

- ☐ Fall (51 WCPM)
- ☐ Winter (72 WCPM)
- ☐ Spring (89 WCPM)

WCPM	÷	Words Read	=	Accuracy %

PROSODY

	L1	L2	L3	L4
Reading in Phrases	O	O	O	O
Pace	O	O	O	O
Syntax	O	O	O	O
Self-correction	O	O	O	O
Intonation	O	O	O	O

Let's Ski!

Many children ski. It is fun to ski in the snow.

Children dress to stay warm.

They dress to stay dry.

Snow is very cold. It is wet.

They wear goggles.

These keep snow out of their eyes.

Children use small skis. They are easy to use.

First they go down small hills. They don't go fast.

They practice a lot on small hills.

Later they jump over small bumps.

It is fun to ski over bumps of snow.

Adults must be near when children ski.

Adults make sure no one gets hurt. Let's ski!

✓ What do goggles do?

✓ Who needs to be close when children ski?

Name: _____   Date: _____

Let's Ski!

11	Many children ski. It is fun to ski in the snow.
16	Children dress to stay warm.
21	They dress to stay dry.
28	Snow is very cold. It is wet.
31	They wear goggles.
38	These keep snow out of their eyes.
47	Children use small skis. They are easy to use.
57	First they go down small hills. They don't go fast.
64	They practice a lot on small hills.
70	Later they jump over small bumps.
79	It is fun to ski over bumps of snow.
86	Adults must be near when children ski.
95	Adults make sure no one gets hurt. Let's ski!

 What do goggles do?

 Who needs to be close when children ski?

Words Read	-	Errors	=	WCPM

☐ **Fall (51 WCPM)**
☐ **Winter (72 WCPM)**
☐ **Spring (89 WCPM)**

WCPM	÷	Words Read	=	Accuracy %

PROSODY				
	L1	L2	L3	L4
Reading in Phrases	O	O	O	O
Pace	O	O	O	O
Syntax	O	O	O	O
Self-correction	O	O	O	O
Intonation	O	O	O	O

Mandy and Paul

Mandy always plays ball with Paul.

They like to play on the lawn.

Mandy is six and Paul is four.

Mandy throws the ball to Paul.

The ball flies past Paul. It goes into the street.

Paul runs to get the ball.

Mandy calls, "No, Paul! Don't get the ball!

Stay on the lawn!"

Mandy runs to stop Paul.

She grabs his arms. She sticks to him like glue!

Mandy makes Paul stop.

Mom and Dad run outside.

"Nice job, Mandy!" Mom says. "You saved Paul!"

"I always want Paul safe," Mandy says.

✓ What are Mandy and Paul doing?

✓ How does Mandy help Paul?

Name: _____ Date: _____

Mandy and Paul

6	Mandy always plays ball with Paul.
13	They like to play on the lawn.
20	Mandy is six and Paul is four.
26	Mandy throws the ball to Paul.
36	The ball flies past Paul. It goes into the street.
42	Paul runs to get the ball.
50	Mandy calls, "No, Paul! Don't get the ball!
54	Stay on the lawn!"
59	Mandy runs to stop Paul.
69	She grabs his arms. She sticks to him like glue!
73	Mandy makes Paul stop.
78	Mom and Dad run outside.
86	"Nice job, Mandy!" Mom says. "You saved Paul!"
93	"I always want Paul safe," Mandy says.

 What are Mandy and Paul doing?

 How does Mandy help Paul?

Words Read	-	Errors	=	WCPM

☐ **Fall (51 WCPM)**
☐ **Winter (72 WCPM)**
☐ **Spring (89 WCPM)**

WCPM	÷	Words Read	=	Accuracy %

PROSODY				
	L1	L2	L3	L4
Reading in Phrases	O	O	O	O
Pace	O	O	O	O
Syntax	O	O	O	O
Self-correction	O	O	O	O
Intonation	O	O	O	O

Firefighters

The firefighters wait in the station.

They are ready for a fire.

The alarm goes off! It is very loud.

The firefighters put on jackets.

The jackets will keep them safe.

Then they jump into the fire truck.

The lights on the truck turn on. The siren blasts.

It is loud so that other cars will clear the way.

The firefighters race to the fire.

Someone gave 911 the address.

The truck can get to the fire fast.

The firefighters work to stop the heat and fire.

They have a special hose. It puts the fire out.

Firefighters save lives.

✔ Why is the fire truck siren so loud?

✔ How do firefighters know there is a fire?

Name: _____ Date: _____

Firefighters

6	The firefighters wait in the station.
12	They are ready for a fire.
20	The alarm goes off! It is very loud.
25	The firefighters put on jackets.
31	The jackets will keep them safe.
38	Then they jump into the fire truck.
48	The lights on the truck turn on. The siren blasts.
59	It is loud so that other cars will clear the way.
65	The firefighters race to the fire.
70	Someone gave 911 the address.
78	The truck can get to the fire fast.
87	The firefighters work to stop the heat and fire.
97	They have a special hose. It puts the fire out.
100	Firefighters save lives.

 Why is the fire truck siren so loud?

 How do firefighters know there is a fire?

Words Read	-	Errors	=	WCPM

☐ **Fall (51 WCPM)**
☐ **Winter (72 WCPM)**
☐ **Spring (89 WCPM)**

WCPM	÷	Words Read	=	Accuracy %

PROSODY				
	L1	L2	L3	L4
Reading in Phrases	O	O	O	O
Pace	O	O	O	O
Syntax	O	O	O	O
Self-correction	O	O	O	O
Intonation	O	O	O	O

Joan's Daydream

Joan did not want to play hopscotch.

But Maria said it would be fun.

Maria threw the first stone.

The stone landed on the first square.

Maria hopped over that square. Joan watched.

But Joan did not pay much attention.

She started to daydream.

Joan looked at squares. She watched Maria hop.

Wherever Maria hopped, flowers sprouted up!

Maria kept hopping. More flowers grew.

The flowers grew taller and taller.

Soon the hopscotch court was a jungle!

Joan heard a voice.

It came from deep in the jungle.

It was Maria's voice!

She was telling Joan that it was her turn.

✔ What are Joan and Maria playing?

✔ How can the reader tell that Joan is daydreaming?

Name: _____ Date: _____

Joan's Daydream

7	Joan did not want to play hopscotch.
14	But Maria said it would be fun.
19	Maria threw the first stone.
26	The stone landed on the first square.
33	Maria hopped over that square. Joan watched.
40	But Joan did not pay much attention.
44	She started to daydream.
52	Joan looked at squares. She watched Maria hop.
58	Wherever Maria hopped, flowers sprouted up!
64	Maria kept hopping. More flowers grew.
70	The flowers grew taller and taller.
77	Soon the hopscotch court was a jungle!
81	Joan heard a voice.
88	It came from deep in the jungle.
92	It was Maria's voice!
101	She was telling Joan that it was her turn.

 What are Joan and Maria playing?

 How can the reader tell that Joan is daydreaming?

Words Read	-	Errors	=	WCPM

☐ **Fall (51 WCPM)**
☐ **Winter (72 WCPM)**
☐ **Spring (89 WCPM)**

WCPM	÷	Words Read	=	Accuracy %

PROSODY				
	L1	L2	L3	L4
Reading in Phrases	O	O	O	O
Pace	O	O	O	O
Syntax	O	O	O	O
Self-correction	O	O	O	O
Intonation	O	O	O	O

All Kinds of Holidays

Holidays are fun.

There are many different holidays.

One holiday, we give thanks for what we have.

Families share special meals.

What is this celebration called?

On another special day, there are parades.

There are lots of floats.

There are fireworks at night.

What is that holiday called?

Another holiday celebrates veterans.

People make speeches.

We remember veterans.

What is this day called?

Have you heard of a holiday called Arbor Day?

People plant new trees in dirt.

They try to help Earth.

What is your favorite holiday?

✔ Which holiday in the article is MOST LIKELY July 4th?

✔ What do people do on Arbor Day?

Name: _____ Date: _____

All Kinds of Holidays

3	Holidays are fun.
8	There are many different holidays.
17	One holiday, we give thanks for what we have.
21	Families share special meals.
26	What is this celebration called?
33	On another special day, there are parades.
38	There are lots of floats.
43	There are fireworks at night.
48	What is that holiday called?
52	Another holiday celebrates veterans.
55	People make speeches.
58	We remember veterans.
63	What is this day called?
72	Have you heard of a holiday called Arbor Day?
78	People plant new trees in dirt.
83	They try to help Earth.
88	What is your favorite holiday?

 Which holiday in the article is MOST LIKELY July 4th?

Which holiday in the article is MOST LIKELY July 4th?

What do people do on Arbor Day?

Words Read	-	Errors	=	WCPM

☐ **Fall (51 WCPM)**
☐ **Winter (72 WCPM)**
☐ **Spring (89 WCPM)**

WCPM	÷	Words Read	=	Accuracy %

PROSODY				
	L1	L2	L3	L4
Reading in Phrases	O	O	O	O
Pace	O	O	O	O
Syntax	O	O	O	O
Self-correction	O	O	O	O
Intonation	O	O	O	O

Carly in the Dark

My name is Carly.

I'm a smart kid, but I don't like the dark.

It doesn't matter if I am very tired.

As soon as Mom turns out the light, I'm awake.

Poor me! I pull my blanket up to my chin.

Then I look around my room.

Shapes seem to creep out of the walls.

I shout, "Mom!"

Mom says that the dark can play tricks.

"It's just car lights shining inside," she says.

Still, it's hard to sleep. So Mom has a plan.

She will get me a night-light. She's so smart!

Now I will sleep through the night.

✔ What is Carly's problem?

✔ How does Mom solve the problem?

Name: _____ Date: _____

Carly in the Dark

4	My name is Carly.
14	I'm a smart kid, but I don't like the dark.
22	It doesn't matter if I am very tired.
32	As soon as Mom turns out the light, I'm awake.
42	Poor me! I pull my blanket up to my chin.
48	Then I look around my room.
56	Shapes seem to creep out of the walls.
59	I shout, "Mom!"
67	Mom says that the dark can play tricks.
75	"It's just car lights shining inside," she says.
85	Still, it's hard to sleep. So Mom has a plan.
95	She will get me a night-light. She's so smart!
102	Now I will sleep through the night.

 What is Carly's problem?

 How does Mom solve the problem?

Words Read	-	Errors	=	WCPM

- ☐ Fall (51 WCPM)
- ☐ Winter (72 WCPM)
- ☐ Spring (89 WCPM)

WCPM	÷	Words Read	=	Accuracy %

PROSODY

	L1	L2	L3	L4
Reading in Phrases	O	O	O	O
Pace	O	O	O	O
Syntax	O	O	O	O
Self-correction	O	O	O	O
Intonation	O	O	O	O

Elephants and Their Trunks

Baby elephants drink milk.

But soon they will find their own food.

Elephants have trunks. Trunks are like long noses.

A trunk grabs things. It picks them up.

Trunks are useful.

Trunks help elephants get food.

Baby elephants learn to use them.

Elephants eat leaves and fruit.

But these are high in the trees.

Trunks can help. They can reach high branches.

Elephants need water.

A trunk is helpful here, too.

Elephants suck water into their trunks.

They bring the trunks to their mouths.

They drink the water from their trunks.

✓ What do elephants eat?

✓ How do trunks help elephants?

Name: _____ Date: _____

Elephants and Their Trunks

4	Baby elephants drink milk.
12	But soon they will find their own food.
20	Elephants have trunks. Trunks are like long noses.
28	A trunk grabs things. It picks them up.
31	Trunks are useful.
36	Trunks help elephants get food.
42	Baby elephants learn to use them.
47	Elephants eat leaves and fruit.
54	But these are high in the trees.
62	Trunks can help. They can reach high branches.
65	Elephants need water.
71	A trunk is helpful here, too.
77	Elephants suck water into their trunks.
84	They bring the trunks to their mouths.
91	They drink the water from their trunks.

☑ What do elephants eat?

☑ How do trunks help elephants?

Words Read	-	Errors	=	WCPM

☐ Fall (51 WCPM)
☐ Winter (72 WCPM)
☐ Spring (89 WCPM)

WCPM	÷	Words Read	=	Accuracy %

PROSODY

	L1	L2	L3	L4
Reading in Phrases	O	O	O	O
Pace	O	O	O	O
Syntax	O	O	O	O
Self-correction	O	O	O	O
Intonation	O	O	O	O

Lady and Spike

We have two pets. We have a cat and a dog.

Our dog's name is Lady. Her fur is white.

Our cat's name is Spike. His fur is black.

Lady likes to chase balls. She chases her tail.

Spike chases mice. Spike naps a lot.

People think dogs and cats are not friends.

That is not always true.

Lady and Spike are very good friends.

Sometimes they clean each other.

Spike licks Lady's ears.

Sometimes they play together.

Lady will roll a ball to Spike.

They like to nap together on the mat.

✔ What does Spike like to do?

✔ How are Spike and Lady different from other cats and dogs?

Name: _____ Date: _____

Lady and Spike

11	We have two pets. We have a cat and a dog.
20	Our dog's name is Lady. Her fur is white.
29	Our cat's name is Spike. His fur is black.
38	Lady likes to chase balls. She chases her tail.
45	Spike chases mice. Spike naps a lot.
53	People think dogs and cats are not friends.
58	That is not always true.
65	Lady and Spike are very good friends.
70	Sometimes they clean each other.
74	Spike licks Lady's ears.
78	Sometimes they play together.
85	Lady will roll a ball to Spike.
93	They like to nap together on the mat.

 What does Spike like to do?

How are Spike and Lady different from other cats and dogs?

Words Read	-	Errors	=	WCPM

☐ **Fall (51 WCPM)**
☐ **Winter (72 WCPM)**
☐ **Spring (89 WCPM)**

WCPM	÷	Words Read	=	Accuracy %

PROSODY				
	L1	L2	L3	L4
Reading in Phrases	O	O	O	O
Pace	O	O	O	O
Syntax	O	O	O	O
Self-correction	O	O	O	O
Intonation	O	O	O	O

People Need Trees

Trees give people food to eat.

Fruits grow on trees. Apples come from trees.

Oranges and bananas do, too.

Trees give us wood. It is used for many things.

Wood makes good homes for people.

Some things in homes are made of wood.

Tables and chairs are made of wood.

Many toys are, too.

Trees also give us paper. Wood is cut into chips.

The wood chips are made into pulp.

Pulp is soft and wet. The pulp is pressed thin.

Then it dries into paper.

Trees are good for the air, too.

They keep the air clean. Trees are very helpful!

✔ Name two things for which wood is used.

✔ How is paper made?

Name: _____ Date: _____

People Need Trees

6	Trees give people food to eat.
14	Fruits grow on trees. Apples come from trees.
19	Oranges and bananas do, too.
29	Trees give us wood. It is used for many things.
35	Wood makes good homes for people.
43	Some things in homes are made of wood.
50	Tables and chairs are made of wood.
54	Many toys are, too.
64	Trees also give us paper. Wood is cut into chips.
71	The wood chips are made into pulp.
81	Pulp is soft and wet. The pulp is pressed thin.
86	Then it dries into paper.
93	Trees are good for the air, too.
102	They keep the air clean. Trees are very helpful!

 Name two things for which wood is used.

 How is paper made?

Words Read	-	Errors	=	WCPM

☐ **Fall (51 WCPM)**
☐ **Winter (72 WCPM)**
☐ **Spring (89 WCPM)**

WCPM	÷	Words Read	=	Accuracy %

PROSODY

	L1	L2	L3	L4
Reading in Phrases	O	O	O	O
Pace	O	O	O	O
Syntax	O	O	O	O
Self-correction	O	O	O	O
Intonation	O	O	O	O

My Photo Album

I am looking at photos in my photo album.

This picture is from last spring.

I am standing with my mom and my dad.

We are about to get on an airplane.

We are going to see my grandparents.

This is my sister, Kim. Kim is five.

Here I am with Kim. We are standing by a lake.

The big, brown dog is Shaw.

In this picture, Shaw jumps into the lake.

He was soaked when he came out.

I had to dry him off.

There is more to see, but it is time for bed.

✓ When did the narrator take a plane ride?

✓ Who is Shaw?

Name: _____ Date: _____

My Photo Album

9	I am looking at photos in my photo album.
15	This picture is from last spring.
24	I am standing with my mom and my dad.
32	We are about to get on an airplane.
39	We are going to see my grandparents.
47	This is my sister, Kim. Kim is five.
58	Here I am with Kim. We are standing by a lake.
64	The big, brown dog is Shaw.
72	In this picture, Shaw jumps into the lake.
79	He was soaked when he came out.
85	I had to dry him off.
96	There is more to see, but it is time for bed.

 When did the narrator take a plane ride?

 Who is Shaw?

Words Read	-	Errors	=	WCPM

☐ **Fall (51 WCPM)**
☐ **Winter (72 WCPM)**
☐ **Spring (89 WCPM)**

WCPM	÷	Words Read	=	Accuracy %

PROSODY

	L1	L2	L3	L4
Reading in Phrases	O	O	O	O
Pace	O	O	O	O
Syntax	O	O	O	O
Self-correction	O	O	O	O
Intonation	O	O	O	O

A Family of Bears

Bears live in places called *dens*.

Baby bears are called *cubs*.

The cubs live with their mother.

The cubs are little.

They do not to go outside.

They run and play in the den.

The mother bear hunts for food.

Then she brings it to the den.

The cubs get bigger.

Their mother shows them how to hunt.

They look for mice and fish.

They search for nuts and ants.

They catch bugs called *grubs*.

They think that bugs are yummy!

✔ Why do cubs stay in dens?

✔ What do cubs eat?

Name: _____ Date: _____

A Family of Bears

6	Bears live in places called *dens*.
11	Baby bears are called *cubs*.
17	The cubs live with their mother.
21	The cubs are little.
27	They do not to go outside.
34	They run and play in the den.
40	The mother bear hunts for food.
47	Then she brings it to the den.
51	The cubs get bigger.
58	Their mother shows them how to hunt.
64	They look for mice and fish.
70	They search for nuts and ants.
75	They catch bugs called *grubs*.
81	They think that bugs are yummy!

 Why do cubs stay in dens?

 What do cubs eat?

Words Read	-	Errors	=	WCPM

☐ **Fall (51 WCPM)**
☐ **Winter (72 WCPM)**
☐ **Spring (89 WCPM)**

WCPM	÷	Words Read	=	Accuracy %

PROSODY				
	L1	L2	L3	L4
Reading in Phrases	O	O	O	O
Pace	O	O	O	O
Syntax	O	O	O	O
Self-correction	O	O	O	O
Intonation	O	O	O	O

The Wright Brothers

The Wright brothers were inventors.

The both of them dreamed of flying.

They hoped to build a flying machine.

Both brothers were curious as children.

They liked to see how things worked.

As grownups, they worked in a bike shop.

The Wright brothers built a glider.

This glider was very light. It had two wings.

Each wing was covered with cloth.

They tested their glider. It flew like a kite.

After the test, one brother got on the glider.

He glided in the air.

The Wright brothers made many gliders.

They tested each one.

Their gliders got better with every test.

Each one stayed in the air longer and longer.

✔ What was the Wright brothers' dream?

✔ Where did the Wright brother work?

Name: _____ Date: _____

The Wright Brothers

5	The Wright brothers were inventors.
12	The both of them dreamed of flying.
19	They hoped to build a flying machine.
25	Both brothers were curious as children.
32	They liked to see how things worked.
40	As grownups, they worked in a bike shop.
46	The Wright brothers built a glider.
55	This glider was very light. It had two wings.
61	Each wing was covered with cloth.
70	They tested their glider. It flew like a kite.
79	After the test, one brother got on the glider.
84	He glided in the air.
90	The Wright brothers made many gliders.
94	They tested each one.
101	Their gliders got better with every test.
110	Each one stayed in the air longer and longer.

 What was the Wright brothers' dream?

 Where did the Wright brother work?

Words Read	-	Errors	=	WCPM

☐ **Fall (51 WCPM)**
☐ **Winter (72 WCPM)**
☐ **Spring (89 WCPM)**

WCPM	÷	Words Read	=	Accuracy %

PROSODY	L1	L2	L3	L4
Reading in Phrases	O	O	O	O
Pace	O	O	O	O
Syntax	O	O	O	O
Self-correction	O	O	O	O
Intonation	O	O	O	O

The Pet Show

Last week, we put on a pet show.

It was at the Tate School in Ms. Hale's class.

Gale came with a fish, and Eric brought his dog.

Daniel came with a snake. Jane had a frog.

"His name is Wade," said Jane. "He is the best!"

"Why?" Gale asked.

Then Wade jumped up.

Jane yelled, "Get Wade!"

We all helped, but Jane's frog got away.

Where did Wade end up?

We looked under desks; we looked in the hall.

Then we found him. He was inside the fish tank!

Ms. Hale located a net and scooped up Wade.

She said, "Everyone, hold on to your pets!"

✔ How can the reader tell that Jane likes Wade?

✔ Why is Wade hard to find?

Name: _____ Date: _____

The Pet Show

8	Last week, we put on a pet show.
18	It was at the Tate School in Ms. Hale's class.
28	Gale came with a fish, and Eric brought his dog.
38	Daniel came with a snake, and Jane had a frog.
48	"His name is Wade," said Jane. "He is the best!"
51	"Why?" Gale asked.
55	Then Wade jumped up.
59	Jane yelled, "Get Wade!"
67	We all helped, but Jane's frog got away.
72	Where did Wade end up?
81	We looked under desks; we looked in the hall.
91	Then we found him. He was inside the fish tank!
100	Ms. Hale located a net and scooped up Wade.
108	She said, "Everyone, hold on to your pets!"

 How can the reader tell that Jane likes Wade?

 Why is Wade hard to find?

Words Read	-	Errors	=	WCPM

☐ **Fall (51 WCPM)**
☐ **Winter (72 WCPM)**
☐ **Spring (89 WCPM)**

WCPM	÷	Words Read	=	Accuracy %

PROSODY				
	L1	L2	L3	L4
Reading in Phrases	O	O	O	O
Pace	O	O	O	O
Syntax	O	O	O	O
Self-correction	O	O	O	O
Intonation	O	O	O	O

Wildfires

Wildfires can ruin land.

These fires can damage homes.

They can hurt plants and animals.

Sometimes they hurt people, too.

These fires happen all around the world.

They show up in forests.

They appear in grasslands.

They tend to occur in hot, dry weather.

A wildfire starts like any fire.

It needs oxygen. Oxygen is a gas in the air.

A fire needs fuel. Fuel is something that burns.

Trees and grasses burn quickly. Fire spreads fast.

Wildfires need heat as well.

The heat might come from lightning.

It could come from striking a match.

That is why adults must take care with matches.

✔ What fuel do wildfires use?

✔ What is the MAIN idea of this article?

Name: _____ Date: _____

Wildfires

4	Wildfires can ruin land.
9	These fires can damage homes.
15	They can hurt plants and animals.
20	Sometimes they hurt people, too.
27	These fires happen all around the world.
32	They show up in forests.
36	They appear in grasslands.
44	They tend to occur in hot, dry weather.
50	A wildfire starts like any fire.
60	It needs oxygen. Oxygen is a gas in the air.
69	A fire needs fuel. Fuel is something that burns.
77	Trees and grasses burn quickly. Fire spreads fast.
82	Wildfires need heat as well.
88	The heat might come from lightning.
95	It could come from striking a match.
104	That is why adults must take care with matches.

✔ What fuel do wildfires use?

✔ What is the MAIN idea of this article?

Words Read	-	Errors	=	WCPM

☐ **Fall (51 WCPM)**
☐ **Winter (72 WCPM)**
☐ **Spring (89 WCPM)**

WCPM	÷	Words Read	=	Accuracy %

PROSODY				
	L1	L2	L3	L4
Reading in Phrases	O	O	O	O
Pace	O	O	O	O
Syntax	O	O	O	O
Self-correction	O	O	O	O
Intonation	O	O	O	O

Late for School

Jason sat up in bed and looked at the clock.

It was half past eight. "Oh, no!" he said.

"I overslept, and I will be late for school."

Jason brushed his teeth and got dressed.

He packed his books. His mom called upstairs.

"Come downstairs for your pancakes," she said.

"I can't eat pancakes today!" Jason cried.

"I am very late for school."

"You must eat three pancakes," she said.

"Breakfast is an important meal."

She put three pancakes on Jason's plate.

They were the size of saucers and delicious!

"Thanks, Mom," Jason said, racing out the door.

Then he ran all the way to school.

He sat in his seat just as the bell rang.

◆ What is Jason's problem at the beginning of the story?

◆ How big are the pancakes?

Oral Reading Fluency Assessment

Name: _____ Date: _____

Late for School

10	Jason sat up in bed and looked at the clock.
19	It was half past eight. "Oh, no!" he said.
28	"I overslept, and I will be late for school."
35	Jason brushed his teeth and got dressed.
43	He packed his books. His mom called upstairs.
50	"Come downstairs for your pancakes," she said.
57	"I can't eat pancakes today!" Jason cried.
63	"I am very late for school."
70	"You must eat three pancakes," she said.
75	"Breakfast is an important meal."
82	She put three pancakes on Jason's plate.
90	They were the size of saucers and delicious!
98	"Thanks, Mom," Jason said, racing out the door.
106	Then he ran all the way to school.
116	He sat in his seat just as the bell rang.

 What is Jason's problem at the beginning of the story?

 How big are the pancakes?

Words Read	-	Errors	=	WCPM

☐ **Fall (51 WCPM)**
☐ **Winter (72 WCPM)**
☐ **Spring (89 WCPM)**

WCPM	÷	Words Read	=	Accuracy %

PROSODY				
	L1	L2	L3	L4
Reading in Phrases	O	O	O	O
Pace	O	O	O	O
Syntax	O	O	O	O
Self-correction	O	O	O	O
Intonation	O	O	O	O

Shoes from Long Ago

People have worn shoes for a long time.

Today, some shoes are worn as decoration.

The first shoes were not.

They were worn to protect. They kept feet safe.

Some people lived in cold places.

Their shoes looked like bags of fur.

They were made from the skins of animals.

Others lived in warm places.

They could wear sandals on their feet.

The sandals were made from grass or leather.

There have been many kinds of shoes.

Some of them were funny.

At one time, some men wore quite long shoes.

The front of the shoe had a chain.

It was attached to the man's knee.

Why? This kept him from tripping!

✓ What were the first cold weather shoes like?

✓ Why could people in warm places
wear sandals?

Name: _____ Date: _____

Shoes from Long Ago

8	People have worn shoes for a long time.
15	Today, some shoes are worn as decoration.
20	The first shoes were not.
29	They were worn to protect. They kept feet safe.
35	Some people lived in cold places.
42	Their shoes looked like bags of fur.
50	They were made from the skins of animals.
55	Others lived in warm places.
62	They could wear sandals on their feet.
70	The sandals were made from grass or leather.
77	There have been many kinds of shoes.
82	Some of them were funny.
91	At one time, some men wore quite long shoes.
99	The front of the shoe had a chain.
106	It was attached to the man's knee.
112	Why? This kept him from tripping!

✔ What were the first cold weather shoes like?

✔ Why could people in warm places wear sandals?

Words Read	-	Errors	=	WCPM

☐ **Fall (51 WCPM)**
☐ **Winter (72 WCPM)**
☐ **Spring (89 WCPM)**

WCPM	÷	Words Read	=	Accuracy %

PROSODY	L1	L2	L3	L4
Reading in Phrases	O	O	O	O
Pace	O	O	O	O
Syntax	O	O	O	O
Self-correction	O	O	O	O
Intonation	O	O	O	O

Something Stinks

Carlos and Mark were in the yard after dark.

They were gazing up at the stars.

They had to draw a constellation for their class.

Carlos saw something. It darted across the yard.

"Did you see a black ball just now?" he asked.

Then Mark saw something move, too.

"Did you see that white streak?" he asked.

Carlos asked, "Do you smell something rotten?"

He held his nose as Mark replied, "I sure do."

Mark made a face. He held his nose as well.

They knew what they had seen. It was a skunk!

✔ Where are Carlos and Mark?

✔ How do Carlos and Mark know they saw
a skunk?

Name: _____ Date: _____

Something Stinks

9	Carlos and Mark were in the yard after dark.
16	They were gazing up at the stars.
25	They had to draw a constellation for their class.
33	Carlos saw something. It darted across the yard.
43	"Did you see a black ball just now?" he asked.
49	Then Mark saw something move, too.
57	"Did you see that white streak?" he asked.
64	Carlos asked, "Do you smell something rotten?"
74	He held his nose as Mark replied, "I sure do."
84	Mark made a face. He held his nose as well.
94	They knew what they had seen. It was a skunk!

 Where are Carlos and Mark?

 How do Carlos and Mark know they saw a skunk?

Words Read	-	Errors	=	WCPM

☐ **Fall (51 WCPM)**
☐ **Winter (72 WCPM)**
☐ **Spring (89 WCPM)**

WCPM	÷	Words Read	=	Accuracy %

PROSODY				
	L1	L2	L3	L4
Reading in Phrases	O	O	O	O
Pace	O	O	O	O
Syntax	O	O	O	O
Self-correction	O	O	O	O
Intonation	O	O	O	O

Helicopters Help!

Helicopters are much different than airplanes.

They fly straight up or straight down.

They can fly backward and sideways.

They can even stay in one place.

Planes need a runway. Helicopters do not!

They can land in tight spaces.

Helicopters are used to do many things.

They can rescue people. A rope can be dropped.

Sometimes a big basket is tied to the rope.

This can pick up people below.

Helicopters can pull people from sinking ships.

They can save people from burning buildings.

Helicopters also are used carry things.

They can carry food and medicine.

They take it to places that are hard to reach.

Helicopters help!

✓ How are helicopters different than airplanes?

✓ Name one thing helicopters are used for.

Name: _____ Date: _____

Helicopters Help!

6	Helicopters are much different than airplanes.
13	They fly straight up or straight down.
19	They can fly backward and sideways.
26	They can even stay in one place.
33	Planes need a runway. Helicopters do not!
39	They can land in tight spaces.
46	Helicopters are used to do many things.
55	They can rescue people. A rope can be dropped.
64	Sometimes a big basket is tied to the rope.
70	This can pick up people below.
77	Helicopters can pull people from sinking ships.
84	They can save people from burning buildings.
91	Helicopters also are used carry things.
97	They can carry food and medicine.
107	They take it to places that are hard to reach.
109	Helicopters help!

 How are helicopters different than airplanes?

Name one thing helicopters are used for.

Words Read	-	Errors	=	WCPM

☐ **Fall (51 WCPM)**
☐ **Winter (72 WCPM)**
☐ **Spring (89 WCPM)**

WCPM	÷	Words Read	=	Accuracy %

PROSODY

	L1	L2	L3	L4
Reading in Phrases	O	O	O	O
Pace	O	O	O	O
Syntax	O	O	O	O
Self-correction	O	O	O	O
Intonation	O	O	O	O

Fox and Grapes

One night, Fox had a good dream about grapes.

Fox woke up and thought about his dream.

It's late June, and the weather is hot and sunny.

The grapes are ripe, and I can find them.

Fox set off across the hill where he saw grapes.

They sat way up on vines on tree branches.

Fox went after the tasty grapes.

First, he ran to gain speed. Then he jumped up.

However, he couldn't reach. Fox rose on tiptoes.

But it was still no use; he just couldn't reach.

At last Fox gave up. "This is silly," Fox said.

"I don't want those grapes. They are not great."

☑ What is the moral of this story?

☑ What did Fox dream about?

Name: _____ Date: _____

Fox and Grapes

9	One night, Fox had a good dream about grapes.
17	Fox woke up and thought about his dream.
27	*It's late June, and the weather is hot and sunny.*
36	*The grapes are ripe, and I can find them.*
46	Fox set off across the hill where he saw grapes.
55	They sat way up on vines on tree branches.
61	Fox went after the tasty grapes.
71	First, he ran to gain speed. Then he jumped up.
79	However, he couldn't reach. Fox rose on tiptoes.
89	But it was still no use; he just couldn't reach.
99	At last Fox gave up. "This is silly," Fox said.
108	"I don't want those grapes. They are not great."

 What is the moral of this story?

 What did Fox dream about?

Words Read	-	Errors	=	WCPM

☐ **Fall (51 WCPM)**
☐ **Winter (72 WCPM)**
☐ **Spring (89 WCPM)**

WCPM	÷	Words Read	=	Accuracy %

PROSODY				
	L1	L2	L3	L4
Reading in Phrases	O	O	O	O
Pace	O	O	O	O
Syntax	O	O	O	O
Self-correction	O	O	O	O
Intonation	O	O	O	O

Scoring Sheets
and
Answer Keys

Name: _____   Date: _____

WEEKLY ASSESSMENT SCORING SHEET   UNIT __ WEEK __

Item	Content Focus	Score	Comments
1			
2			
3			
4			
5			

Name: _____   Date: _____

MID-UNIT ASSESSMENT SCORING SHEET   UNIT __

Item	Content Focus	Score	Comments
1			
2			
3			
4			
5			
6			
7			
8			
9			
10			

Name: _____ Date: _____

UNIT ASSESSMENT SCORING SHEET UNIT __

Item	Content Focus	Score	Comments
1			
2			
3			
4			
5			
6			
7			
8			
9			
10			
11			
12			
13			
14			
15			

Copyright © McGraw-Hill Education. Permission is granted to reproduce for classroom use.

Assessment · Scoring Sheet

Name: _____ Date: _____

EXIT ASSESSMENT SCORING SHEET   UNIT __

Item	Content Focus	Score	Comments
1			
2			
3			
4			
5			
6			
7			
8			
9			
10			
11			
12			
13			
14			
15			

Weekly Assessment Answer Key

UNIT 1 WEEK 1

Item #	Content Focus
1	Key Details
2	Key Details
3	Vocabulary: Context Clues
4	Vocabulary: Context Clues
5	Key Details

Suggested Responses:

1. **Text Evidence:** Sam is sick.
2. **Text Evidence:** a card
3. **Text Evidence:** If Sam needs him, Fred is there.
4. **Text Evidence:** feels great
5. **Text Evidence:** Sam thanks Fred for the card.

UNIT 1 WEEK 2

Item #	Content Focus
1	Character, Setting, Events
2	Character, Setting, Events
3	Vocabulary: Context Clues
4	Vocabulary: Context Clues
5	Character, Setting, Events

Suggested Responses:

1. Italy
2. **Text Evidence:** Mom and Rick fly on a plane to see Gran. Then they ride a train to Gran's house.
3. **Text Evidence:** They speak a different **language**.
4. **Text Evidence:** He tries new food. Gran shows him art.
5. **Text Evidence:** a week

UNIT 1 WEEK 3

Item #	Content Focus
1	Character, Setting, Events
2	Vocabulary: Context Clues
3	Character, Setting, Events
4	Vocabulary: Context Clues
5	Character, Setting, Events

Suggested Responses:

1. **Text Evidence:** the park
2. **Text Evidence:** looks <u>hard</u> at
3. milk
4. **Text Evidence:** right
5. **Text Evidence:** a cat

UNIT 1 WEEK 4

Item #	Content Focus
1	Key Details
2	Vocabulary: Context Clues
3	Vocabulary: Context Clues
4	Key Details
5	Key Details

Suggested Responses:

1. **Text Evidence:** at the zoo
2. **Text Evidence:** Looking after
3. **Text Evidence:** walk
4. **Text Evidence:** plants
5. kids

UNIT 1 WEEK 5

Item #	Content Focus
1	Key Details
2	Vocabulary: Context Clues
3	Key Details
4	Key Details
5	Vocabulary: Context Clues

Suggested Responses:

1. Dad grows corn.
2. **Text Evidence:** Mom makes the food. She makes pies with fresh fruit.
3. **Text Evidence:** Mom
4. **Text Evidence:** a pie store
5. **Text Evidence:** people in the store

UNIT 2 WEEK 1

Item #	Content Focus
1	Character, Setting, Plot
2	Vocabulary: Context Clues
3	Character, Setting, Plot
4	Vocabulary: Context Clues
5	Character, Setting, Plot

Suggested Responses:

1. **Text Evidence:** His class visits a pond.
2. **Text Evidence:** adjust
3. **Text Evidence:** Their teeth can chop wood.
4. **Text Evidence:** looks forward
5. He will write a report about beavers.

Weekly Assessment · Answer Key

UNIT 2 WEEK 2

Item #	Content Focus
1	Problem and Solution
2	Vocabulary: Context Clues
3	Problem and Solution
4	Problem and Solution
5	Vocabulary: Context Clues

Suggested Responses:

1. **Text Evidence:** Bear could not find food.
2. **Text Evidence:** think
3. **Text Evidence:** He looked near his cave and then all over the woods.
4. Turtle gives Bear food.
5. **Text Evidence:** he must prepare for winter

UNIT 2 WEEK 3

Item #	Content Focus
1	Main Topic
2	Vocabulary: Context Clues
3	Vocabulary: Context Clues
4	Key Details
5	Key Details

Suggested Responses:

1. life in a bay
2. **Text Evidence:** covered
3. **Text Evidence:** a place animals can survive
4. **Text Evidence:** the calm water
5. **Text Evidence:** fish

UNIT 2 WEEK 4

Item #	Content Focus
1	Main Topic
2	Vocabulary: Context Clues
3	Vocabulary: Context Clues
4	Key Details
5	Key Details

Suggested Responses:

1. zebras
2. **Text Evidence:** children
3. **Text Evidence:** fully grown
4. **Text Evidence:** grasses
5. **Text Evidence:** hooves

UNIT 2 WEEK 5

Item #	Content Focus
1	Key Details
2	Literary Elements: Rhythm
3	Key Details
4	Literary Elements: Rhyme
5	Key Details

Suggested Responses:

1. **Text Evidence:** brown
2. **Text Evidence:** cries
3. **Text Evidence:** Pat's friendly face
4. four
5. smiled, and picked her up

Weekly Assessment • Answer Key

UNIT 3 WEEK 1

Item #	Content Focus
1	Author's Purpose
2	Vocabulary: Context Clues
3	Vocabulary: Context Clues
4	Author's Purpose
5	Author's Purpose

Suggested Responses:

1. friction
2. **Text Evidence:** A force is a push or a pull.
3. **Text Evidence:** things
4. **Text Evidence:** Rough surfaces have more friction than smooth surfaces.
5. to explain what friction is and how it affects us

UNIT 3 WEEK 2

Item #	Content Focus
1	Sequence
2	Vocabulary: Context Clues
3	Sequence
4	Sequence
5	Vocabulary: Context Clues

Suggested Responses:

1. **Text Evidence:** in their cabin at camp
2. **Text Evidence:** sounded unhappy
3. **Text Evidence:** Then the boys walked slowly back to their cabin.
4. He wants Bob to see the rainbow.
5. **Text Evidence:** Pleased

UNIT 3 WEEK 3

Item #	Content Focus
1	Author's Purpose
2	Vocabulary: Context Clues
3	Vocabulary: Context Clues
4	Author's Purpose
5	Author's Purpose

Suggested Responses:

1 **Text Evidence:** community gardens

2 **Text Evidence:** thoughts

3 **Text Evidence:** solve the problem

4 **Text Evidence:** how to eat better

5 The author's purpose is to tell people how community gardens are made and why they are good for the community.

UNIT 3 WEEK 4

Item #	Content Focus
1	Main Idea and Details
2	Vocabulary: Context Clues
3	Vocabulary: Context Clues
4	Main Idea and Details
5	Main Idea and Details

Suggested Responses:

1 blizzards

2 **Text Evidence:** rough

3 **Text Evidence:** cause harm

4 **Text Evidence:** more than a day

5 **Text Evidence:** stay safe

Weekly Assessment • Answer Key

UNIT 3 WEEK 5

Item #	Content Focus
1	Main Idea and Key Details
2	Vocabulary: Context Clues
3	Main Idea and Key Details
4	Vocabulary: Context Clues
5	Main Idea and Key Details

Suggested Responses:

1 **Text Evidence:** she opened a ballet school

2 **Text Evidence:** sounds made by instruments

3 **Text Evidence:** 16

4 **Text Evidence:** know

5 **Text Evidence:** Children can express themselves by dancing.

UNIT 4 WEEK 1

Item #	Content Focus
1	Compare and Contrast
2	Compare and Contrast
3	Compare and Contrast
4	Vocabulary: Context Clues
5	Vocabulary: Context Clues

Suggested Responses:

1 **Text Evidence:** Bridal Veil Falls is the smallest waterfall.

2 **Text Evidence:** Three Waterfalls, Two Places

3 They are both in New York.

4 **Text Evidence:** winter and summer

5 **Text Evidence:** not too hot or too cold

UNIT 4 WEEK 2

Item #	Content Focus
1	Vocabulary: Context Clues
2	Cause and Effect
3	Vocabulary: Context Clues
4	Cause and Effect
5	Cause and Effect

Suggested Responses:

1. **Text Evidence:** lively
2. **Text Evidence:** a forest fire starts
3. **Text Evidence:** firm
4. **Text Evidence: Effects of Forest Fires**
5. Different seeds are able to grow.

UNIT 4 WEEK 3

Item #	Content Focus
1	Compare and Contrast
2	Vocabulary: Context Clues
3	Compare and Contrast
4	Vocabulary: Context Clues
5	Compare and Contrast

Suggested Responses:

1. **Text Evidence:** United States
2. **Text Evidence:** go from one place to another
3. Juan knows many more Spanish words than Claire does.
4. **Text Evidence:** We share our food.
5. **Text Evidence:** We like it better than anything!

UNIT 4 WEEK 4

Item #	Content Focus
1	Vocabulary: Context Clues
2	Theme
3	Theme
4	Vocabulary: Context Clues
5	Theme

Suggested Responses:

1 **Text Evidence:** yelled out

2 **Text Evidence:** She flies down and pulls Ant from the water.

3 **Text Evidence:** Eagle helped me before.

4 **Text Evidence:** runs over

5 If you help others, they will help you.

UNIT 4 WEEK 5

Item #	Content Focus
1	Theme
2	Literary Elements: Simile
3	Theme
4	Literary Elements: Alliteration
5	Theme

Suggested Responses:

1 **Text Evidence:** by a tree

2 One day as I sat

3 **Text Evidence:** Stanza 1: by a tree; Stanza 2: by the sea; Stanza 3: under the sun

4 **Text Evidence:** sang, some, special, songs

5 **Text Evidence:** lines 13-14

UNIT 5 WEEK 1

Item #	Content Focus
1	Point of View
2	Vocabulary: Context Clues
3	Vocabulary: Context Clues
4	Point of View
5	Point of View

Suggested Responses:

1. He had oustide activities he wanted to do.
2. **Text Evidence:** "I am definitely going to do everything on this list."
3. **Text Evidence:** problems
4. **Text Evidence:** This sounded like a tough job that could take a long time.
5. **Text Evidence:** My list of activities did not seem so important after all.

UNIT 5 WEEK 2

Item #	Content Focus
1	Vocabulary: Context Clues
2	Point of View
3	Point of View
4	Vocabulary: Context Clues
5	Point of View

Suggested Responses:

1. **Text Evidence:** quiet
2. **Text Evidence:** I'm the best actor in our class.
3. **Text Evidence:** I don't care about this play.
4. **Text Evidence:** work together
5. He thinks the play was a lot of fun.

UNIT 5 WEEK 3

Item #	Content Focus
1	Sequence
2	Vocabulary: Context Clues
3	Sequence
4	Vocabulary: Context Clues
5	Sequence

Suggested Responses:

1 **Text Evidence:** she went to a law school to study

2 **Text Evidence:** She learned many things about the law.

3 Next, Sandra wanted to get a job in a law firm.

4 **Text Evidence:** did very well!

5 **Text Evidence:** 1981

UNIT 5 WEEK 4

Item #	Content Focus
1	Problem and Solution
2	Vocabulary: Context Clues
3	Vocabulary: Context Clues
4	Problem and Solution
5	Problem and Solution

Suggested Responses:

1 **Text Evidence:** "Our baseball field has disappeared!"

2 **Text Evidence:** wanted to learn more

3 **Text Evidence:** doesn't happen often

4 They worked with friends to help clean up the field.

5 **Text Evidence:** They picked up bottles and collected metal cans and paper.

UNIT 5 WEEK 5

Item #	Content Focus
1	Vocabulary: Context Clues
2	Cause and Effect
3	Vocabulary: Context Clues
4	Cause and Effect
5	Cause and Effect

Suggested Responses:

1. **Text Evidence:** They tell what is allowed.
2. **Text Evidence:** they cannot be in the contest
3. **Text Evidence:** after a few days
4. The one who spells the most words right wins the big bee.
5. **Text Evidence:** cannot win

UNIT 6 WEEK 1

Item #	Content Focus
1	Theme
2	Vocabulary: Context Clues
3	Theme
4	Vocabulary: Context Clues
5	Theme

Suggested Responses:

1. **Text Evidence:** The gifts helped the animals survive.
2. **Text Evidence:** came into sight
3. **Text Evidence:** my spots protect me by helping me hide
4. **Text Evidence:** grow
5. Be happy with your gifts.

UNIT 6 WEEK 2

Item #	Content Focus
1	Author's Purpose
2	Vocabulary: Context Clues
3	Vocabulary: Context Clues
4	Author's Purpose
5	Author's Purpose

Suggested Responses:

1. **Text Evidence:** to turn on a light or work on a computer
2. **Text Evidence:** beneath the surface of the Earth
3. **Text Evidence:** the energy that makes lights and machines work
4. **Text Evidence:** Energy from Trash
5. **Text Evidence:** We can use trash to make energy we need.

UNIT 6 WEEK 3

Item #	Content Focus
1	Vocabulary: Context Clues
2	Main Idea and Key Details
3	Main Idea and Key Details
4	Vocabulary: Context Clues
5	Main Idea and Key Details

Suggested Responses:

1. **Text Evidence:** helps them get ready
2. **Text Evidence:** The astronauts work together in extreme conditions.
3. **Text Evidence:** a new animal
4. **Text Evidence:** because of
5. Astronauts need to work as a team.

UNIT 6 WEEK 4

Item #	Content Focus
1	Problem and Solution
2	Vocabulary: Context Clues
3	Vocabulary: Context Clues
4	Problem and Solution
5	Problem and Solution

Suggested Responses:

1 **Text Evidence:** They think pennies do not have any value, or worth.

2 **Text Evidence:** worth

3 They collect pennies for different causes.

4 **Text Evidence:** Students collect pennies and other spare change to help sick kids.

5 **Text Evidence:** $2,000

UNIT 6 WEEK 5

Item #	Content Focus
1	Literary Elements: Beats
2	Point of View
3	Point of View
4	Literary Elements: Metaphor
5	Point of View

Suggested Responses:

1 4

2 **Text Evidence:** I see a shiny rocket ship, submarine

3 **Text Evidence:** amazing

4 **Text Evidence:** box, submarine

5 **Text Evidence:** Look at the fun I can have.

Mid-Unit Assessment Answer Key

UNIT 1

Item #	Answer	Content Focus
1	B	Character, Setting, Events
2	A	Vocabulary: Context Clues
3	B	Key Details
4	C	Key Details
5	C	Character, Setting, Events
6	A	Vocabulary: Context Clues
7	B	Key Details
8	C	Character, Setting, Events
9	B	Vocabulary: Context Clues
10	A	Character, Setting, Events

UNIT 2

Item #	Answer	Content Focus
1	C	Main Topic and Key Details
2	C	Main Topic and Key Details
3	A	Vocabulary: Context Clues
4	B	Vocabulary: Context Clues
5	C	Text Features: Subheadings
6	C	Vocabulary: Context Clues
7	A	Problem and Solution
8	C	Problem and Solution
9	A	Plot
10	B	Plot

UNIT 3

Item #	Answer	Content Focus
1	B	Sequence
2	B	Vocabulary: Context Clues
3	A	Sequence
4	A	Vocabulary: Context Clues
5	A	Sequence
6	A	Vocabulary: Context Clues
7	B	Author's Purpose
8	C	Author's Purpose
9	A	Author's Purpose
10	C	Text Features: Diagram

UNIT 4

Item #	Answer	Content Focus
1	B	Compare and Contrast
2	B	Vocabulary: Context Clues
3	C	Compare and Contrast
4	A	Cause and Effect
5	C	Cause and Effect
6	A	Text Features: Map
7	B	Vocabulary: Context Clues
8	C	Compare and Contrast
9	B	Vocabulary: Context Clues
10	C	Compare and Contrast

Mid-Unit Assessment · Answer Key

UNIT 5

Item #	Answer	Content Focus
1	B	Vocabulary: Context Clues
2	B	Point of View
3	C	Point of View
4	A	Vocabulary: Context Clues
5	A	Point of View
6	A	Sequence
7	B	Vocabulary: Context Clues
8	A	Sequence
9	C	Sequence
10	C	Text Features: Timeline

UNIT 6

Item #	Answer	Content Focus
1	B	Vocabulary: Context Clues
2	C	Main Topic and Key Details
3	C	Main Topic and Key Details
4	B	Text Features: Diagram
5	C	Author's Purpose
6	B	Vocabulary: Context Clues
7	A	Vocabulary: Context Clues
8	A	Theme
9	B	Theme
10	B	Theme

Mid-Unit Assessment · Answer Key

Unit Assessment Answer Key

UNIT 1

Item #	Answer	Content Focus
1	A	Character, Setting, Events
2	C	Character, Setting, Events
3	B	Key Details
4	C	Vocabulary: Context Clues
5	A	Vocabulary: Context Clues
6	B	Character, Setting, Events
7	C	Key Details
8	C	Vocabulary: Context Clues
9	A	Key Details
10	B	Vocabulary: Context Clues
11	A	Key Details
12	C	Key Details
13	A	Key Details
14	B	Key Details
15	C	Vocabulary: Context Clues

UNIT 2

Item #	Answer	Content Focus
1	B	Problem and Solution
2	A	Vocabulary: Context Clues
3	C	Key Details
4	B	Vocabulary: Context Clues
5	A	Key Details
6	C	Problem and Solution
7	B	Plot
8	A	Plot
9	C	Main Topic and Key Details
10	B	Vocabulary: Context Clues
11	C	Vocabulary: Context Clues
12	C	Main Topic and Key Details
13	A	Text Features: Headings
14	B	Main Topic and Key Details
15	C	Vocabulary: Context Clues

UNIT 3

Item #	Answer	Content Focus
1	B	Sequence
2	A	Sequence
3	A	Sequence
4	C	Vocabulary: Context Clues
5	A	Sequence
6	A	Vocabulary: Context Clues
7	B	Sequence
8	C	Main Idea and Key Details
9	B	Author's Purpose
10	C	Text Features: Subheadings
11	C	Vocabulary: Context Clues
12	A	Vocabulary: Context Clues
13	B	Vocabulary: Context Clues
14	A	Main Idea and Key Details
15	C	Author's Purpose

UNIT 4

Item #	Answer	Content Focus
1	A	Theme
2	C	Vocabulary: Context Clues
3	C	Vocabulary: Context Clues
4	B	Compare and Contrast
5	B	Compare and Contrast
6	A	Compare and Contrast
7	C	Theme
8	A	Vocabulary: Context Clues
9	A	Vocabulary: Context Clues
10	A	Compare and Contrast
11	C	Cause and Effect
12	B	Vocabulary: Context Clues
13	C	Compare and Contrast
14	A	Cause and Effect
15	C	Text Features: Map

Unit Assessment • Answer Key

UNIT 5

Item #	Answer	Content Focus
1	C	Problem and Solution
2	B	Vocabulary: Context Clues
3	A	Problem and Solution
4	A	Vocabulary: Context Clues
5	C	Point of View
6	A	Point of View
7	B	Problem and Solution
8	C	Point of View
9	A	Vocabulary: Context Clues
10	A	Cause and Effect
11	C	Sequence
12	A	Vocabulary: Context Clues
13	B	Vocabulary: Context Clues
14	A	Cause and Effect
15	A	Text Features: Timeline

UNIT 6

Item #	Answer	Content Focus
1	C	Vocabulary: Context Clues
2	B	Theme
3	A	Point of View
4	B	Vocabulary: Context Clues
5	A	Point of View
6	C	Point of View
7	A	Author's Purpose
8	B	Vocabulary: Context Clues
9	C	Main Idea and Key Details
10	B	Problem and Solution
11	A	Vocabulary: Context Clues
12	B	Problem and Solution
13	C	Vocabulary: Context Clues
14	A	Author's Purpose
15	B	Text Features: Bar Graph

Unit Assessment · Answer Key

Exit Assessment Answer Key

UNIT 1

Item #	Answer	Content Focus
1	C	Vocabulary: Context Clues
2	B	Character, Setting, Events
3	A	Character, Setting, Events
4	B	Vocabulary: Context Clues
5	B	Key Details
6	C	Vocabulary: Context Clues
7	A	Character, Setting, Events
8	C	Key Details
9	B	Vocabulary: Context Clues
10	A	Key Details
11	A	Key Details
12	C	Key Details
13	B	Key Details
14	A	Key Details
15	B	Vocabulary: Context Clues

UNIT 2

Item #	Answer	Content Focus
1	C	Plot
2	B	Plot
3	A	Problem and Solution
4	B	Key Details
5	C	Vocabulary: Context Clues
6	A	Problem and Solution
7	C	Vocabulary: Context Clues
8	C	Main Topic and Key Details
9	A	Main Topic and Key Details
10	C	Vocabulary: Context Clues
11	A	Main Topic and Key Details
12	A	Main Topic and Key Details
13	B	Text Features: Chart
14	B	Vocabulary: Context Clues
15	A	Vocabulary: Context Clues

UNIT 3

Item #	Answer	Content Focus
1	A	Sequence
2	B	Vocabulary: Context Clues
3	C	Sequence
4	B	Vocabulary: Context Clues
5	C	Sequence
6	A	Sequence
7	B	Sequence
8	C	Vocabulary: Context Clues
9	B	Main Topic and Key Details
10	C	Vocabulary: Context Clues
11	A	Author's Purpose
12	C	Text Features: Diagram
13	A	Main Topic and Key Details
14	B	Vocabulary: Context Clues
15	C	Author's Purpose

UNIT 4

Item #	Answer	Content Focus
1	C	Vocabulary: Context Clues
2	A	Cause and Effect
3	C	Cause and Effect
4	A	Compare and Contrast
5	B	Compare and Contrast
6	A	Vocabulary: Context Clues
7	C	Text Features: Subheadings
8	A	Vocabulary: Context Clues
9	A	Vocabulary: Context Clues
10	C	Theme
11	B	Compare and Contrast
12	A	Compare and Contrast
13	B	Vocabulary: Context Clues
14	A	Theme
15	B	Theme

Exit Assessment · Answer Key

UNIT 5

Item #	Answer	Content Focus
1	B	Point of View
2	C	Vocabulary: Context Clues
3	A	Problem and Solution
4	C	Vocabulary: Context Clues
5	C	Problem and Solution
6	A	Problem and Solution
7	A	Point of View
8	B	Vocabulary: Context Clues
9	B	Cause and Effect
10	A	Cause and Effect
11	B	Vocabulary: Context Clues
12	C	Sequence
13	A	Sequence
14	B	Text Features: Chart
15	C	Vocabulary: Context Clues

UNIT 6

Item #	Answer	Content Focus
1	C	Problem and Solution
2	C	Vocabulary: Context Clues
3	B	Vocabulary: Context Clues
4	A	Main Idea and Key Details
5	B	Author's Purpose
6	C	Text Features: Diagram
7	B	Main Idea and Key Details
8	C	Vocabulary: Context Clues
9	A	Author's Purpose
10	A	Point of View
11	B	Vocabulary: Context Clues
12	B	Point of View
13	C	Vocabulary: Context Clues
14	B	Theme
15	A	Theme